C000147608

Question. Seek. Become.

The Processes of Spiritual Awakening & Enlightenment

For More Information or to Contact the Author:

www.MichealHarding.com

Facebook: AuthorMichealHarding

Instragram: @MettaHostel

Also by Micheal Harding:

To see this gangly kid with glasses at family events growing up, Micheal seemed to be nothing but normal. He played with his many cousins, he stuffed his face with sweets, and he laughed and laughed and laughed. But what no one knew, what no one could know, was that it was <u>only</u> at these events over his <u>entire</u> childhood that Micheal was not humiliated, hunted and tortured.

The results? Chronic depression and addiction from the age of twelve lasting for four decades. And then a complete mental breakdown at the age of thirty-nine and a violent showdown with law enforcement.

His is a tragic tale of endless suffering, a childhood robbed, and a constant darkness of both mind and spirit.

Available on Amazon.

Dedicated to all who seek truth.

Contents

Introduction

Most people live their entire lives not knowing that spiritual awakening and enlightenment are the birthright of every single human being ever born on this planet and can be attained completely outside of orthodoxy and orthopraxy <u>and</u> in a single lifetime.

No child in any modern society is taught that they are the best person to lead their own self-healing, awakening and enlightenment, nor are they freely provided with the tools that are available today to do so, the jagged pieces of which are clutched possessively in the hands of orthodoxies and orthopraxies around the world and throughout history. The Buddha, one of the very few fully enlightened beings to be noted in history, is quoted by some to have told his own monks to "Work out your own salvation. Do not depend on others".

Yet in this technological age, the only place that we

can fetter out any path to awakening and enlightenment today lies with others, namely orthodoxy and orthopraxy, and its always their way or the highway.

Like many of you, I have scoured pages, monitors and minds for most of my life, trying to find what was missing within myself. Every single human being tries to fill that emptiness or void within with something, anything really. The only thing that differs in us is the degree to which we clue into that fact. But the one thing that we all know for sure is that we each are lacking something, or at least we always feel that we are lacking something. Is it a thing, a person, a place or a state of being? It varies between who you ask and during which rotation around the sun you ask them. But we all have that core yearning. It is the quintessential human quality.

Thus from first breath, every human being ever born seeks to fill that void, and the tribe is always too happy to comply. Most humans go their entire lives without questioning their tribal, societal, religious, national, or cultural conditioning, being so completely sold on those prepackaged interpretations of reality.

However, some do question. It can be the simplest thing really, such as "Why am I not as happy as everyone else seems to be?" And with that simple act of questioning, that predictable, inevitable, perhaps even genetically programmed response blossoms in our chest; we seek. What we seek, we may not know, but we begin to consciously or at least subconsciously seek for something. The tribal conditioning has slipped in one corner of the veil of reality; something incomprehensible was glimpsed for but a moment., and that was enough.

The Seeker within has stirred.

The real challenge for every human being then is that <u>first</u> awakening from merely "<u>s</u>eeking" prepackaged concepts to fill that hard drive called a brain in order to survive and prosper in the tribe, to being what most authorities on the subject refer to as a "Seeker", or one who seeks ultimate truth.

Seeking and awakening to all the great truths that our souls have all forgotten as part of the deal of experiencing all the highs and lows of biological life should be the first goal of every being born on this planet. This should be fully supported by both church and state and made learnable for free by anyone, anywhere, anytime, from any country, of any culture, of any language, of any religion, or of no religion at all.

But that is not our reality.

Awakening and enlightenment are not taught in schools because it is largely considered a religious issue, and orthodoxy and orthopraxy will only provide what information they have on spiritual awakening and enlightenment to those followers who unquestioningly and wholeheartedly accept the organizationally constructed and approved world view, which includes how awakening and enlightenment are defined, and how an enlightened person thinks, acts, and lives.

And one can hardly be blamed for presuming that with the state of technology as advanced as it is, combined with nearly five thousand years of orthodoxy and orthopraxy development around the world on the subjects of awakening and enlightenment, it should be fairly straight forward and reasonably attainable for the average person of reasonable intelligence to be able to locate everything they need to know about the processes involved, what to expect, and how to navigate sub-processes like partial awakening.

Not so.

In past generations, Seekers had to venture to the corners of the world and the fringes of belief systems to find information even remotely usable in forging a path to awakening and enlightenment. Technology has not made things easier, and in all likelihood has probably made things much harder.

There is so much information online that it would take a lifetime to note and organize, much less go through, interpret and apply. Every religion, every way of life, every different branch and lineage, and even every leader and instructor in those different those branches and lineages seems to have their own take on awakening and enlightenment, the stages and categories involved, what happens during the processes, what is required to make it happen and what it all means. What is more, the information fluctuates greatly and is inevitably buried beneath orthodoxy and orthopraxy editorializing.

My own spiritual journey spanned three continents, four decades, five belief systems and countless conversations, until one day I realized where all the answers had been all along. And with that vital realization, things really picked up speed for me, for from that day I became, and still am, a willing participant on the journey to full spiritual enlightenment.

The following pages contain a collection of information including definitions, stages, symptoms, warnings and suggestions regarding awakening and enlightenment that I have collected over the last three decades as well as from recent online scans. Most religious information originates in some way from the big five of religion Buddhism, Christianity, Hinduism, Islam, and Judaism), with some references to Sufism and Wicca. The main orthopraxy source was Buddha-Dharma, and I have added supportive information throughout from well-known contemporary and historical minds and noted online and literature sources in the <u>Sources</u> section at the end of the book.

Everything was then filtered to remove extraneous or "fringe" information and religious or organizational editorializing that orthodoxies and orthopraxies can not help but weave in, so that we are left with simply information. From there, duplication has been eliminated, relevant and common terms, definitions, stages and categories have been merged, and modern language and contemporary research findings were added where available and relevant.

This is not a deep research piece, nor is it a scholarly article to be peer-reviewed. I am a process person, both in terms of work experience and the way that my mind works, and so my sole intention was to gather together in one easy-to-read and to-the-point reference document as much useful information about the processes involved with spiritual awakening and enlightenment as I've both collected over my journey and found online.

May you find something that lies within helpful.

Chapter 1: Awakening

"Your vision will become clear only when you can
look into your own heart.
Who looks outside, dreams; who looks inside,
awakes." – Carl Young

What does it mean to spiritually awaken?

This question has been much debated since human beings first learned how to debate. Wherever one turns to pose this question of orthodoxy (religion, or a way of believing) or orthopraxy (a way of living), one will receive a wide variety of responses.

For example, the Catholic Encyclopedia with newadvent.org offers that spiritual awakening can be related to the illuminative way:

> "The illuminative way is that of those who are in the state of progress and have their passions better under control, so that they easily keep themselves from mortal sin, but

who do not so easily avoid venial sins, because they still take pleasure in earthly things and allow their minds to be distracted by various imaginations and their hearts with numberless desires, though not in matters that are strictly unlawful. It is called the illuminative way, because in it <u>the mind becomes more and more enlightened as to spiritual things and the practice of virtue</u> [underline added]."

We can see that newadvent.org recognizes a journey of some kind to awakening ("...the mind becomes <u>more and more</u> enlightened... [underline added]"), and that on this journey, progress is made in matters of emotions (referred to as "passions").

In his book titled <u>Indian Buddhism</u> (2000), A. K. Warder states that in Buddhism, awakening is described as being synonymous with Nirvana, the extinction of the <u>passions</u> [underline added; note the similar wording above], whereby suffering is ended and no more rebirths in this world need take place. Warder specifically notes that the insight arises in the person in which this awakening is occurring:

> "Knowledge arose in me, and insight: my freedom is certain, this is my last birth, now there is no rebirth."

Just as in Catholicism, Buddhism recognizes spiritual awakening as a process in which knowledge arises in a person gradually over time, though some Buddhists believe that this can take many lifetimes to realize.

Ibn Qayyim al-Jawziyya, a late twelfth century Sunni Imam, who was an important medieval Islamic theologian and spiritual writer is often quoted:

> "The first of the ranks of the journey of servitude is awakening, which is alarming and stirring up of the heart from the sleep of heedlessness...Whoever experiences it, by Allah, he has indeed experienced the breeze

of success. Without experiencing it, everyone is lost in heedlessness. His hearing is asleep while his eyes appear awake. It is this blessed alarm that wakes one up and makes him a seeker of Allah. The seeker now rolls up his sleeves and musters up his courage to set out on the journey to Allah, station by station."

Other Islamic thinkers also recognize that awakening is only the beginning of a journey, and the person who experiences such an awakening must bravely seek out Allah (God), which again suggests that the full process happens over time.

Many Hindu definitions for enlightenment (called "Moksha") refer to a talk by a strong supporter of the Upanyasam type of Hinduism, Sri B. Sundarkumar. He said that according to Hindu scriptures, enlightenment is actually the deep understanding of the truth of Brahman (God) as an experience in one's awareness at all times, and this leads to eternal life. Such a matured soul has reached the highest level of spiritual growth in which the being becomes one with all reality. This takes controlling the creation of karma and resolving past karmas, and the process is only complete when the soul is fully matured in the knowledge of these holy laws and follows them in all things. Sundarkumar words can be understood to say that Hindu scriptures as recognize different levels of spiritual growth, which strongly suggests that spiritual growth and awakening is a process, though Hindus believe that it can take many lifetimes to complete.

Outside of orthodoxy, in their highly insightful book titled The Spiritual Awakening Process, Aletheia Luna and Mateo Sol speak to spiritual awakening:

> "There comes a moment in our lives where we grow out of the collective values and ways of living common to our societies. At

a certain point in our lives, we realize that the values, attitudes, relationships, and beliefs we've held no longer contribute to the development of who we truly are; our authentic selves."

"For centuries, the indigenous peoples throughout the world have known that to explore the depths of the Soul fully, we must venture into a spiritual journey of the unknown darkness within ourselves. In many ancient cultures, there were Elders and Shamans to encourage and oversee these quests toward a deeper spiritual existence."

Another non-religious definition of awakening comes from a modern source, Catherine G. Lucas, author, mindfulness instructor and Founding Director of the UK Spiritual Crisis Network, who often speaks on the subject of mental and spiritual emergencies and runs workshops on mindfulness and spirituality:

> "So what is spiritual awakening? It is above all a process; a process of exploration and unfolding; a process of learning and growth, of healing and purification. It involves the whole of our being and works on all levels, physical, emotional and psychological, as well as spiritual."

In her amazingly insightful book titled <u>Learning About Spiritual Awakenings: 2 Young Crones Library Book 9</u>, Elizabeth Chapman, who had a strong Wiccan background, said this about awakening:

> "Awakening allows the continual sacred space to have your own personal <u>Truth</u> revealed. Being truthful allows you to get in touch with your authenticity, able to feel your body as an indicator of what feels true for you. When you begin to live in alignment with your Truth, genuine love

emerges through your spiritual Awakening."

Finally, author and PhD Psychologist Bonnie Greenwell states that spiritual awakening is "the waking up of consciousness to the remembrance of its original nature".

For now and for our purposes, we need to arrive at a common understanding of what awakening is and what it involves. There is a lot of information in this issue, and naturally it needs to be filtered and condensed. To start with, everything was filtered to remove "fringe" information which was supported by few or no other sources. Next, religious and organizational editorializing that orthodoxies and orthopraxies can not help but weave in was washed out. From there, duplication was eliminated, relevant and common terms, definitions, stages and categories were merged, and modern language and contemporary research findings were added where available and relevant. We will refer to this process moving forward as applying the "Filter".

After applying the "Filter" to the data collected, this is what we are left with:

> "Awakening" is above all a process involving at first spiritual unrest, then seeking, then healing, and finally the realizing of ultimate truth, or full awakening. There are many stages to awakening, and there are different types of awakenings that can occur together or completely separate from each other. Awakening may take place over several lifetimes but can be completed in a single lifetime and may result in reaching full spiritual enlightenment (defined later in chapter 4).

Partial vs Full Awakening

Information available today has a number of different terms and meanings for this concept. Some talk about it as temporary/permanent awakening, others as non-abiding/abiding awakening, with a large number of sources unhelpfully suggesting that if a person undergoes only a temporary/non-abiding/partial awakening, that they have somehow failed. That they have somehow been fooled into believing in a story that was not true, or that they have fallen into a trap that they could have avoided, and even that they could have fully awakened, had things gone a different way, none of which is very accurate.

The concepts that we will refer to moving forward as partial and full Awakening simply represent the idea that any person that experiences a spiritual awakening will either experience a full and instant awakening, or they will not.

What is implied here, but often missed, is that the person can also land anywhere in between being zero and fully awake, which means that there are most simply three states of awakening: fully unawakened ("Unawakened"), partially Awakened or fully Awakened.

If the Awakening is of the "instant" kind, the Seeker will one moment not fully understand a specific knowledge or life area (referred to moving forward as a "facet" of Awakening), and the very next moment, they will fully understand that same previously unknown knowledge or life area and can apply it to their current situation.

However, the Awakening only <u>seems</u> instant to the human mind.

Awakening will only appear to occur in an instant because it happens too fast for the human brain to follow, but any fully Awakened being will still have gone though <u>all</u> the stages of Awakening, but the stages will have finished in order so quickly, as quick as the blink of an eye, as to have <u>appeared</u> to the limited human senses as having all occurred at exactly the same time.

Additionally, no person starts the process of Awakening to enlightenment in the exact same place and with the exact same knowledge and life experience, and so the whole process, whatever that involves, <u>must</u> take various lengths of time to complete for different people. Some Awakenings take a short amount of time (milliseconds), others take a longer amount of time (decades). But they <u>all</u> take a period of time.

Following this, when a full spiritual awakening does not occur "instantaneously" or in a single instant, it does not mean that the person has failed or fallen short in any way, it simply means that their particular Awakening experience is not of the instant variety, but of the non-instant variety. When the person has absorbed all the information from their life experiences needed for their brain to be able to finish the Awakening, then the process of Awakening will complete itself.

If a person has only a partial Awakening, what can/should they do?

If one does not Awaken in the blink of an eye, they

do not need to try "awaken again" or start the awakening process over again, they simply have to continue to breathe.

Taking longer to Awaken is as normal and as expected as every human body being a different weight at birth. It does <u>not</u> mean that the person has failed, or that full Awakening cannot be reached for that person, but in fact suggests the exact opposite; that Awakening is possible for the Seeker, if they just continue to do what they are doing.

This idea is supported by Steven Taylor, a well-known UK author and lecturer on spirituality and psychology, who did a study of 161 temporary [partial] awakenings (Steven Taylor, 2012b). He found that the people in the study had three different levels of awakening, and that each level had different signs.

In a low-level awakening, called by Taylor a "low intensity awakening", a person may simply have an odd feeling that their environment, their world around them, or perhaps the very fabric of reality itself, has become a little dislodged or see through, even if only for a moment.

In a "medium intensity awakening", a person may have a sudden sense of being one with everyone and/or everything.

> "The person may feel part of this oneness, realizing that he or she is not a separate and isolated ego. He or she may feel a strong sense of compassion and love for others, recognizing that other people are part of the same spiritual ground as them."

In a "high intensity awakening", the whole world may dissolve away into an ocean of spiritual happiness, and the person may sense both the universe and their own soul.

Taylor says though that in all variations of partial awakening, the experience <u>faded</u> after some time. According to an earlier study (Greeley's (1974)), 21% of [partial] awakening experiences lasted for more than a day, 19% of the experiences lasted between ten and thirty minutes, while 37% lasted for only few minutes or less.

American author and spiritual teacher Adyashanti comes at the issue of partial vs full awakening from a different angle. He says that after going through a partial awakening, one person may have 10% of their learned view, or understanding of reality, or understanding of a certain part of reality (called "conditioning" from this point) permanently changed, while another person may have 90% of their conditioning permanently changed. Others can be anywhere in between. It is hard to say why awakening affects one person's conditioning one way and another person's another way. In all cases though, the person's previous conditioning returned in varying amounts.

Adyashanti offers some really good news though. He reports that once a partial awakening has taken place:

"...the aperture of our awareness can never completely close down again. It may seem like it has closed down completely, but it never quite does. In the deepest part of yourself, you don't ever forget. Even if you've only glimpsed reality for a moment, something within you is changed forever."

Awakening Triggers

Taylor's study found that 78% of awakenings were accidental or seemingly for no reason, rather than produced by spiritual practice. Likely things or events that set off the awakening, called triggers, included strong emotional unrest (23.6%), nature (18%), meditation (13%) and watching or listening to an arts performance (13%).

Less likely triggers were found to be mental or emotion changes due to taking drugs such as LSD or magic mushrooms, purposefully not falling asleep or eating for many days, or taking part in a creative performance or athletic activity.

Around 7% of awakenings had no apparent trigger.

What happens during an Awakening?

Adyashanti describes awakening in his book titled The End of Your World: Uncensored Straight Talk on the Nature of Enlightenment:

> "Spiritual awakening is a remembering. It is not becoming something that we are not. It is not about transforming ourselves. It is not about changing ourselves. It is a remembering of what we are, as if we'd known it long ago and had simply forgotten."

Most information sources on the subject of awakening agree that an awakening is a shift in life view, where one realizes that they are not a thing, or a person, or even a separate being, and their sense that they and the world are separate fades.

We will use Adyashanti's definition above of awakening from this point forward.

How does life change after an Awakening?

Many advise that people that experience an awakening most often lose more than they gain, in the beginning at least. They can not only lose their sense of self and who they thought that they were, but their entire view or understanding of their family, friends, their community, their workplace, their country, the world or even life itself shifts.

Dr. Bruce Davis, Director of the <u>Silent Stays Retreat Centre</u> in Napa Valley, California, writes in his book titled <u>Life After a Spiritual Awakening:</u>

> "In a spiritual awakening, colours are more bright, thoughts are more clear, the filter of the mind has been put aside, opening true awareness. During the experience, doubts, worries, desires, hopes and problems, all the debris normally floating in and clogging the mind are gone...life is not about the big things which our minds ponder, but the little ways we lift one another. The good life after

a spiritual awakening is to remember to turn inward again and again for the answers, and more important, the pure substance which makes life worth living. Here we are reminded we are a soul."

After an Awakening, there will always be a time during which the brain sorts out what it has experienced and then works it into, or integrates it, into everyday life. This can happen over a short amount of time, hours or days, or may take weeks or more, depending on the person.

In his book titled <u>Spiritual Theory of Everything A Unique Blueprint to Discover the Origin and Purpose of Life, Awaken Your Consciousness and Lead a Blissful Life</u>, spiritual scientist, teacher and author Thomas Vazhakunnathu says this about awakening:

> "As a person becomes awake (comes out of the conditioned mind), there comes a realization that he is not a 'physical being'

but a 'soul, a 'metaphysical being', presently experiencing life as a human being with the help of a physical body. This realization will cause him to look within instead of searching outside and find the power and presence of his soul."

His book also gives us one of the most well-rounded lists of the most common changes that people that have experienced an awakening can feel afterwards:

An Internal Feeling of Change: Most people that experience an awakening will sense on a very deep mental and emotional level that something has changed inside them. They may feel more comfortable with who they are. They may feel less stress in their everyday life, or they may adopt a calmer attitude about life in general.

An Increased Inspiration: After an awakening, people often find that they are creatively inspired in new and different ways. Completely new and out-of-the-box ideas, sometimes called "radical solutions", for problems that have bothered them for years may suddenly pop into their head. Changes in relationships, job or how they spend their spare time may take place.

An Increased Awareness of Coincidences: People that have experienced an awakening may suddenly become more in tune with the world around them. Not only may they develop an awareness of the chance events in their lives, but there may seem to be more of them happening.

A Better Understanding of and Acceptance of Self: During awakening, most people will have caught a glimpse deep within their mind and had a strong and sudden understanding of great truth about themselves, and then become more accepting of both good and bad parts of themselves.

<u>More Understanding and Accepting of Others</u>: Those who have experienced an awakening may also gain a better understanding of what it means to be human and may find that they are more accepting of flaws in others.

<u>Altruism</u>: Those who experience an awakening may become more active with volunteer work, they may become more emotionally giving in personal relationships, or may help friends, family and even strangers without expecting anything in return.

<u>A Desire to Make the World A Better Place</u>: With the deep understandings of an awakening can come a desire to share that new understanding with the world. They may get involved with social causes,

changes jobs or careers or come up with or take part in projects in their community.

<u>A Desire for More Spiritual Growth</u>: Most often, people who have caught a glimpse of true reality without their ego getting in the way develop a desire for more truth and spiritual growth. They may often suddenly seek out teachers of both orthodoxy or orthopraxy, read books on the subjects of spiritually or self-improvement, or seek the help of mental heath professionals or spiritual advisors.

And finally, Thomas Vazhakunnathu wisely advises this:

> "Once we consciously enter the path of spirituality, there comes a sense of purpose, security, freedom, and abundance in life. We will be able to consciously co-create with nature whatever we choose. Life becomes peaceful and happy as we always find

ourselves being helped and supported by both physical and metaphysical worlds. Even when there is chaos all around, we will be able to maintain calmness and remain unaffected. We will have the capacity to manage painful or difficult situations, smoothly and gracefully because the mind is calm and peaceful."

Chapter 2: The Stages of Awakening

The Stages of Awakening

There is no end to lists from related and truthful sources on the stages of awakening. Most seem to agree though that awakening is a process that occurs in stages that can be defined. Some lists go as high as fifteen, though most settle at either seven or five.

Putting the most common and sensible information through our Filter, the following five stages of Awakening were produced:

Stage 1 – The Dark Night of the Soul

> "There can be no rebirth without a dark night of the soul, a total annihilation of all that you believed in and thought that you were." - Hazrat Inayat Khan

The phrase "dark night of the soul" is the title of a

poem by 16th-century Roman Catholic mystic San Juan de la Cruz, otherwise known as Saint John of the Cross. The poem describes the anguish of the separation of a person's soul from God and was written while de la Cruz was put in prison by the Catholic Church for his different religious beliefs.

This is the stage of Awakening that most every human being that has ever lived has felt at some point in their life, though few would have understood its source. This stage could be expected to begin sometime past puberty and anytime through adulthood, and can often happen as result of a big life event, though author and Ph.D. psychotherapist Bonnie Greenwell advises in her book titled The Awakening Guide: A Companion for the Inward Journey that children can experience partial or full spiritual awakenings:

> "Sometimes this pull begins in childhood, with a persistent wondering about the nature of things. Even at a very early age we can

have gentle openings and understandings about the universal connection between all beings, followed by disappointment when it is seen that adults don't understand this perspective."

Similar ideas exist in different fields of religion, mythology and psychology, and have been noted to include "existential crisis", "soul loss", "descent to the underworld" and may include forms of depression and anxiety.

The Dark Night of the Soul makes most people who go though it feel hopeless or unhappy with the world around them. By this time, the person will be fully conditioned into the tribal culture of their family, community, religion, region and nation. But as the person begins to think for themselves instead of using the pre-made conditioned thinking that they got from the tribe, the person can begin to wonder whether their understanding of the world, or of reality itself, is correct or not.

When this happens, it can be said that the "veil of delusion" may appear to slip. The word "delusion" is used here instead of the word "illusion" because an illusion comes from outside of oneself, from an outside source, like a magician, and in a delusion, the source of the delusion, or at least part of the source, is the person themselves, or some belief, understand or view that they hold.

What this means is that someone that experiences the Dark Night of the Soul may get a short glimpse of a different or deeper view or understanding of the world and their role or place in it. These glimpses can be related to different areas of the person's life which may be in turmoil, such as self-identity, expanding and changing personal relationships, education, employment or religion and/or belief systems on which they have built all meaning in their life.

As they begin to accomplish the big moments in life that society promises will make everyone happy, like buying the brand name clothes, the fancy watches and jewellery, the house, two cars, an attractive or successful partner, a yoga body and so on, some people begin to sense something. What exactly they sense they may not be able to say, but they sense something regardless, and more importantly, they <u>know</u> that they sense something. Perhaps it is just a gut feeling that things may not be exactly the way that they should be, or they may experience a very short altered state of mind or awareness, or even a loss of sound judgment, or maybe a sudden and mysterious distrust in authority, or even the thought that the person doesn't know who they really are or what their purpose in life is — or maybe they have everything that they ever wanted and they find themselves still unhappy, or worse, more unhappy.

People who experience these things all react differently at this point, based off of any one of an infinite number of combinations of genes, family situation and life experience, but most react along the following lines:

a. they completely ignore the experience and they actively distract themselves from future such experiences,

b. they completely ignore the experience, and they continue on in their life as if they had noticed nothing,

c. they continue on in their life, but they remain open to similar experiences,

d. they begin to actively inquire into the nature of their experience,

e. they Awaken partially,

f. they Awaken fully, or

g. they instantly attain full enlightenment.

Its important to note that there are not only six ways people can react, but that they can react between one extreme and the other or <u>anywhere</u> in between. The more that their identity is based on their belief system or lifestyle, the more resistance a person will have to the power of the initial and any following Awakenings, if they occur. If brief moments of awakening do continue to occur (there are no guarantees), the person may eventually begin to focus on them, or they may never notice another waver in the fabric of their reality again.

The Dark Night of the Soul can last a lifetime.

Signs of Partial Awakening

As a person's view of reality begins to waver, the Unawakened can become affected by political and religious extremism. The person's understanding or perception of reality is flickering, but they have not yet seen clearly behind the veil of delusion, and so they are very open to suggestion from others that seem to know what they are talking about. Right at the time that the person is feeling the Dark Night of the Soul and grasping at the straws of their conditioned delusions, a ready-made belief system that the ego can simply slide into place without the need for expending a great amount of energy can be very attractive.

Helpful Approaches

Perhaps it is Adyashanti that says it best:

> "Proper contemplation must occur in the context of radical honesty."

Unless a person is able to be totally honest with themselves one hundred percent of the time, they will not be able to complete the last stage of the awakening process, integrating or working their new knowledge into their everyday life. When one wants to change their behaviour or their thinking, the ability to be honest with themselves is critical. If one lies to oneself, even a simply lie, this means that the person is trying to fool themselves, and this can be a sign of mental illness, and the person may be delusional, or to put it another way, they may delude themselves, or purposefully not look at the truth.

Real and long-lasting changes cannot be made this

way.

Being one hundred percent honest, or radically honest and truthful with oneself, is vital to moving and progressing along the path of true spirituality for any person. If a person cannot recognize and fully admit within themselves the truth of what is for them, or their Truth, then that person must be deluding themselves on some level. Any delusion within a person prevents Awakening and enlightenment, for delusion is the killer of Truth.

The purest love is created through pure truth. When one lives truth, pure love flows through their entire body, both from within themselves for themselves, and from any other source of love on the planet and in the universe. A person can find complete liberation in living in total honesty every day. Relationships become chances to develop wholesome skills, such as being honest and purposeful in everything that they do with another person. The person releases all fear of rejection and moves past the ego and into the heart.

When one lives their Truth, they feel peace within their body, their stress levels drop, and energy is freed to heal old wounds and experience true vitality. The human body thrives on truth and begins to die in the face of any form of delusion.

It will go without saying from this point on that total, complete and radical honesty is vital for every stage of Awakening.

In addition to living one's Truth, meditation generally helps the best with progress in this stage, but any practice in which the person creates focus can be beneficial. These may include yoga, Tai Chi and journaling. Even simply reminding oneself that they are going through the awakening process can also be a great help in finding meaning to hold onto again.

Guidance from trained professionals and/or spiritual advisors can be significantly helpful.

Guidance from someone who has made this journey can be valuable, but it is important to keep in mind that each journey will be unique and so it is vital to not have expectations.

Support from like-minded people can be helpful, such in those a meditation or mindfulness group called a "sangha".

Stage 2 – Changing Perspectives

If in Stage 1, a person's tribal conditioning or "veil of delusion" begins to waver, then in Stage 2 the person begins to see <u>through</u> the veil to something unexpected beyond. Depending on which knowledge or life area the person may be Awakening to, they start to perceive certain parts, aspects or facets of themselves, other people, the world or even reality itself in a new way, and their beliefs, views and understandings of their current reality start to shift or waver.

For instance, the person may begin to see through

the lies or untruths that other people around them say and believe and what the person is actually seeing. The sleeper may become unhappy, and they may become aware of the suffering of people around them, or the suffering of animals or of nature and the environment. The sleeper may begin to feel hopeless to the ills of the world and feel that there is nothing that they can do about any of it.

As in Stage 1, people experiencing a shift in their beliefs and world views in this stage most often react in one of the following ways:

- they completely ignore the experience and they actively distract themselves from future such experiences,

- they completely ignore the experience, and they continue on in their life as if they had noticed nothing,

- they continue on in their life, but they remain open to similar experiences,

51

- they begin to actively inquire into the nature of their experience,

- they Awaken partially,

- they Awaken fully, or

- they instantly attain full enlightenment.

As long as the person remains open to similar experiences, they may continue to move forward on the path of Awakening, but the mind's resistance to change cannot be underestimated.

Billions of beings have been able to do so for their entire lives.

Signs of Partial Awakening

As in Stage 1, the Unawakened are still prone to "perception substitution" where they simply discard the old belief system and replace it with whatever is being offered by someone that seems wiser on the ways of the world, such as conspiracy theorists, fascist groups or cults.

More importantly in this stage though, if a person continues to struggle to ignore or escape their Awakening experience rather than "leaning into it" or allowing it to happen naturally, this avoidance behaviour can become a core pattern of delusion that runs almost completely in the background of the person's mind and would be almost completely unnoticeable.

Helpful Approaches

As the life views that the ego has carefully built around the Unawakened person begin to waver and fall apart, confusion can set in. Learning to accept confusion as a normal emotion can help the person a great deal. If confusion is viewed as a friend simply warning one that they need to pay attention to something important, it becomes less of something that one automatically avoids.

Up until now, the Unawakened person has been maintaining two main types of delusions in their life; the image that the ego has carefully weaved around the Unawakened for the benefit of the outside world (ex: I am desirable, I am generous, etc.), and the delusions or expectations that others in the life of the person have been actively building around the Unawakened person for their own purposes (ex: parents, spouse, best friend, etc.).

As some or all of these delusions begin to fall apart, the person should be fearless and lean into what is happening in their mind, rather than looking away. By looking away at this point, the person continues to deny reality. By leaning in, the person begins to Awaken.

Guidance from trained professionals and/or spiritual advisors can be very helpful.

Guidance from someone who has made this journey can be valuable, but it is important to keep in mind that each journey will be unique, and so it is vital for the person going through an Awakening to not develop expectations.

Support from like-minded people can be helpful,

such in those a meditation or mindfulness group called a "sangha".

Meditation generally helps, but any practice in which the person creates focus can be of benefit.

Stage 3 – Seeking & Gaining Insights

The majority of the information located on the stages of awakening have these two subject areas as separate, but seeking and then gaining insights are really two sides of the same coin. As one seeks, insight is gained. One naturally follows the other.

If a person reaches this stage of Awakening, they begin to actively seek for answers and meaning in their life, and they are recognized almost across the board of the big five as now being a seeker of ultimate truth, or a "Seeker", and they begin to move towards Awakening and enlightenment, though they may or may not consciously realize or understand this at the time.

Now, the real work of Awakening begins.

Seeking

Once a person becomes a willing participant in pulling back the veil of their own reality, they become a Seeker, and this cannot be undone. What has been seen cannot be unseen. This is not to say that the Seeker's enlightenment is all but assured, quite the opposite in fact. The truth is that many Seekers never make it past this point, but without spending a lot of energy, the person never forgets that reality is not what it seems, nor do they forget that they have glimpsed behind it.

The Seeker now actively engages the outside world in trying to discover answers to questions growing within, or to fill the voids they are noticing within. They may start reading books on psychology, philosophy, spirituality, self-help, self-improvement, self-healing, etc. The Seeker may join or float between different social groups, religious groups or mental health professionals in their search for both answers and a place in which they feel "comfortable", or like they "belong".

It is common in this stage for Seekers to seek out teachers of both orthodoxy and orthopraxy, and/or they may leave their home and begin to travel nationally or internationally in search of something that they cannot explain, and which many never find.

Gaining Insights

As the Seeker seeks, they find. They begin to realize smaller truths and experience breakthroughs in certain areas or facets of thought, understanding and life perspective. These truths and breakthroughs can come on gradually within the mind of the Seeker, or they may experience a sudden understanding revealing great truth, otherwise known as "epiphanies".

During this stage, conditioned delusions begin to fade, and the suffering of the awakening person lessens considerably as the Seeker begins to understand more and more about the nature of reality. The awakening Seeker will begin to sense a growing or expanding of something within themselves, and will often feel great happiness, hope, a deeper connection to the people and world around them and may also begin to experience a certain awe with life, the universe and existence in general.

Once a piece of understanding and knowledge has been integrated into their daily life by the Seeker, they go back to seeking (either knowingly or unknowingly) for any additional great or ultimate truths that must be known in order to fully awaken.

Signs of Partial Awakening:

Chasing After "the Light": This is just another way of saying "shutting away the Darkness", which is a common reaction at this stage where the awakening Seeker begins to label things that come up as good or bad, and then actively avoids the bad in a misguided effort to avoid negative people, things and feelings in their life. True spiritual awakening is about being open to the full human experience of all emotions, for it is only the ego that names them and "good" or "bad".

Chasing After Happiness: Similar to chasing after only the good or the light, at this stage Seekers can often get fooled by their ego into thinking that the goal of their recent partial Awakening was the happiness that they felt after. In the days, weeks and possibly even months after their Awakening experience, many Seekers feel physically, mentally and spiritually "lighter", or "better", or "happier". However, as must happen with all people who have not yet fully Awakened, their happiness or temporary bliss naturally fades, and many assume that, as with anything else in life, the happiness has completely and permanently disappeared, and so they go back to old patterns of behaviour in order to get it back.

Positive Thinking: When a person begins actively searching for something and focuses all of their waking attention on getting it, one can do pretty much anything. This is the very real power of positive thinking, often called the "law of attraction", which was made into a cultish movement in recent decades by a book/video series called "The Secret".

As a Seeker starts to really ask about the Truth of themselves and of the reality around them, they generally start to have sudden deep insights as information and data flows into their more and more focused mind. Because each human experience is special and unique, every Seeker will receive information and data in a different order, and so each awakening experience will also be unique.

As we already know, Awakening can occur "instantly", that is, in such a short time as to appear to have occurred instantly in human perception. When this happens though, a single event is not really happening, but rather the Seeker is going through all of the necessary stages that they need to go through in order to achieve full awakening in an extremely small amount of time, which can be in milliseconds.

But in those Awakenings that are "non-instantaneous" or do not occur instantly, the full awakening process can take minutes, hours, days, weeks, months, years or lifetimes. If the Seeker has sudden understanding about the law of attraction before they Awaken to truths relating to materialism or the nature of the mind, then what can result may be what happened after The Secret hit the international markets. The great majority of people used their limited understanding of this power of the mind to generate happiness by changing the world around themselves; they used the power to create financial wealth, to obtain fancy things, to help them become more physically attractive, and so on.

However, as schoolofteachingmastery.com points out, multiple psychologists have debunked The

Secret and the permanency of the success of the law of attraction and positive thinking. They tell us that material possessions only account for about 10% of overall happiness, and this boost only happens for a short time and can actually do a person more harm than good.

Disenfranchisement: In any process, progress is not always in a straight line. That is not how humans work. There is always forward progress followed by a time where the Seeker almost seems to go backwards in their thinking, life views and behaviour. What is actually happening here is that the brain is working overtime to try to integrate the insights recently gained into it's existing understanding and view of the universe and reality.

"Disenfranchisement" or becoming "disenfranchised" or unhappy with something or someone happens when an awakening person begins to feel bored with their new teachers or practices, or they may feel that they are only scratching the surface of something far greater than they expected and/or are ready for.

The Seeker may also have gone through sustained periods of bliss or happiness before this, only to once again feel separated, unhappy and confused.

A Sense of Superiority: As a Seeker gains knowledge and insights, their suffering will go down in different amounts and for different periods of time. As this happens, a Seeker will more easily be able to notice suffering in other people and will naturally feel compassion for them and may even desire to help them.

This desire to help others can often be ego-driven, as any superior-feeling Seeker will have misunderstood one or more of the following things by this point:

- that the Seeker is in a higher intellectual/ethical/moral/spiritual/develop mental position to judge what another completely separate person being needs in order to grow or evolve as a human being or soul,

- that the behaviour in the other person that the Seeker is trying to change is not a core and/or vital defence mechanism for that person,

- that the Seeker's judgment about this person is correct when the Seeker only has a small portion of the total information available about this person's entire life,

- that the other person needs help,

- that the person wants help,

- that the Seeker has enough experience in advising people to be able to change the other person's behaviour in the way that the Seeker wants to, and

- that the Seeker's help, whether wanted or not, would result in the changes that the Seeker wants.

Basically, what happens is that the Seeker begins to believe that with great knowledge comes great responsibility, and that they can and have the responsibility and the resources to help another person to Awaken, just like the Seeker did or is doing.

Emptiness & Loss of Meaning: As the Seeker receives information and data from life around them, their life views and understandings of reality actually changes as they live life, or "on the fly". One day, they simply discover that they are free from the ego's desire to find meaning in everything, including life itself.

Adyashanti says it wonderfully of the experience of the Seeker at this point in their awakening in his book titled The End of Your World: Uncensored Straight Talk on the Nature of Enlightenment:

> "They see that the ego's desire to find meaning in life is actually a substitute for the perception of being life itself. The search

for meaning in life is a surrogate for the knowledge that we are life. Only someone who is disconnected from life itself will seek meaning. Only someone disconnected from life will look for purpose.

When there is a true realization, when we wake up from the dream state, we realize that to search for meaning is no longer appropriate. When we have a direct connection with life, all of a sudden, the quest for meaning and purpose seems rather paltry and insignificant. It is no longer a motivator in our life. The drive for meaning and purpose dissolves because we are coming from a different perspective, a perspective where such things don't really exist, certainly not in the old way. They no longer exist from an egoic standpoint.

The "me," or the ego, can set itself up as the witness. Initially, this can feel tremendously freeing, especially for people who have experienced a lot of pain and suffering in life. All of a sudden, they are the witness, and there is extraordinary relief in no longer being identified as the main character in their life. But the position of the witness can become a fixation, and when it does, a sense of dryness can start to creep in. In this situation, the witness sees itself as unconnected with what is being witnessed. This means, of course, that there hasn't been a true and thorough realization. It is more like a half realization; it's like being halfway awake."

Helpful Approaches

At this early point on their path to enlightenment, the Seeker may be still suffering from many of the delusions of their tribal conditioning. We all grew up through linear, rational, and narrow-minded thinking. Awakening and enlightenment suggest a different view or perception of life, one where it is not the tribe that provides a ready-made belief system to the Seeker, who then simply plugs it into their brain like a video game. Instead, Awakening suggests to the Seeker that they are responsible for their own belief system, ideas, opinions, and viewpoints. However, the problem that can develop is that the existing tribal beliefs and views often get in the way and prevent the Seeker from gaining new wisdom because they are held prisoner by their original and current tribal thinking or conditioning.

Buddhism presents this idea or concept very well. The Buddha (if he was a real person) taught that conceptual thinking is a function of one of five factors that make up and explain a person's personality. The Buddha called it "knowledge that links together." When the human brain learns something new, such as a new idea or concept, it first links the new concept to an already existing concept, something that it has already mapped out in the brain, which in the short term is helpful in learning new knowledge and navigating through unfamiliar mental events.

However, this creates some difficulty when a new concept is linked to an already existing concept which is a result of tribal conditioning and contributes to the person's delusional view of reality. Hence, when an Awakening being is learning new, wholesome concepts that result in a truer perception of reality, most often the Seeker has to unlearn current concepts before a new concept can be understood wholly and integrated or worked into their daily life successfully.

This unlearning process is often referred to as "Emptying the Cup" and is a term that stands for a spiritual concept or idea that is believed to have been first used in a conversation between Chinese Zen Master Ryutan and student Tokusan sometime in the early ninth century.

Seekers at this Stage benefit considerably by emptying their cup and forgetting everything that they know and that they think they know about themselves, human beings, the world and even reality itself. They must unlearn everything that they have ever been taught.

And when their cup is truly empty, they will be ready to receive ultimate truths.

It is also helpful for the Seeker to remind themselves at this point that Awakening isn't about becoming a perfect being. Awakening is about seeing the divisions and roots of those divisions within oneself, for it is exactly the things that divide us on the inside that needs to be examined and healed.

> "We don't come to Nirvana by avoiding Samsara. We don't come to heaven by avoiding hell or trying to sidestep it. We don't come to clarity by avoiding confusion. We don't come to freedom by avoiding that which is less than freedom. The truth is quite the opposite. "- Adyashanti

However, not avoiding confusion is not enough, according to Korean Zen Master Seung Sahn, who advised students to actively cultivate what he called the "don't-know mind":

> "Human beings have too much understanding. Too much understanding, too much have problems. Little bit understanding, little problem. If you don't know, no problem! That's the point: if you don't know, no problem. So Don't-Know mind is very important.
>
> Much understanding means somebody's idea; it's somebody's idea that makes problems for me. Many desires, cannot get the desires, then get angry, then ignorance appears, make ignorant actions – stupid actions. So then you have problems. So Buddha is teaching us, you must attain your true self. If I ask you, "Who are you?", what do you say? You know what I mean?

> Human beings have much understanding, but don't understand anything!"

Meditation can help with sitting with feelings of disenfranchisement and unhappiness. While that may seem a little backward, meditation can help the Seeker train their mind to stop avoiding negative feelings and emotions of all kinds and rather welcome them. The Seeker must at some point come to the realization or understanding that negative feelings and emotions are a vital part of the human mind; in a self-aware being, they point to areas within the mind that require specific attention.

In short, negative feelings and emotions point to areas of Awakening within the Seeker. To avoid them is a form of delusion and will prevent further progress along the path of awakening to enlightenment.

Helpful Approaches

Guidance from trained professionals and/or

spiritual advisors can be very helpful.

Guidance from someone who has made this journey can be valuable, but it is important to keep in mind that each journey will be unique, and so it is vital for the person going through an Awakening to not develop expectations.

Support from like-minded people can be helpful, such in those a meditation or mindfulness group called a "sangha".

Meditation generally helps, but any practice in which the person creates focus can be of benefit.

Stage 4 – Delving Deeper

If the Seeker is successful in Stage 3 in learning and working great truths into their daily life, it likely means that they have learned to sit with all experience without favouritism. Each experience in life is unique and one-of-a-kind, and so there should be appropriate awe with each moment.

The Seeker may recall how their Dark Night of the

Soul was seemingly banished when they turned inward for answers, and so they return to their seeking at this point, but with much more excitement. They may become a serious and devoted practitioner of meditation, mindfulness or prayer. They may want to resolve childhood traumas, to make wholesome changes to certain parts of their personality or physical body, or any other number of wholesome personal development practices.

Once a Seeker reaches Stage 4, they merely need to continue doing exactly what they are doing to complete their awakening, either in this life or the next.

Stage 5 – Complete Integration

If a Seeker arrives at this stage or point in their spiritual growth, they then become fully awake in one specific knowledge or life area, which we will refer to from now on as a "facet" of Awakening. This means that the Seeker will have fully and permanently worked in or integrated the lessons learned from their realization(s) of great truth into their everyday life.

Bliss and connectedness with everything and everyone around them are likely to return, and life and living becomes fuller.

The Seeker returns to seeking the ultimate truths of any remaining facets of Awakening.

Chapter 3: The Facets of Awakening

The Facets of Awakening

Christianity Today says that there are five stages of awakening, and in the different stages the awakening person realizes great truths about longing, regret, seeking help, love and life. Other sources provide similar lists of varying lengths. However, these are not really <u>stages</u> but rather <u>categories</u> or types of awakening.

This idea of different categories or "types" of awakening is supported by late author Elizabeth Chapman in her book titled <u>Learning About Spiritual Awakenings: 2 Young Crones Library Book 9</u>:

> "...we can experience a spiritual awakening in various parts of our lives at different times and through different processes."

Elizabeth goes on to explain that the overall

awakening process can be viewed "...as a series of smaller awakenings that strengthen us spiritually until we have a much larger awakening that propels our growth in a particular area exponentially and then the process starts all over again [underline added]".

Adyashanti advises that there are two different "levels" of spiritual awakening, the level of mind and the level of heart. When a person awakens at the level of mind, they see that the mind has no actual reality to it. Awakening at the level of the heart means that a person begins to understand that their feelings and emotions do not tell them who and what they are as a person.

Gathering a good number of these lists of categories/areas/levels and applying our Filter, five "facets" of Awakening are produced, which consist of the different life or knowledge areas in which a Seeker must realize great truths and successfully work all of their realizations into their understanding of the nature of reality itself. When a person fully Awakens to all five facets of Awakening, the person has become fully spiritually enlightened.

The Facet of Mind

> "We should come to know that there is more reality and sacredness in a blade of grass than in all of our thoughts and ideas about reality." - Adyashanti

Seekers awakening to this facet gradually or suddenly become aware of their conditioning and see its influence on their beliefs and views of the world around them. This mental programming dissolves in the mind of the Seeker and is replaced with consciousness, and there are no longer any emotional or mental concepts that can surprise or fool the Seeker.

Our Unawakened human sense of self is strongly linked with our feelings and emotions. If we are angry, we say that "I" am angry. If we feel sad, we link our very self with that single emotion. To Awaken to emotion means that the Seeker no longer defines their sense of self from how they feel. They understand very deeply that emotions are only a product of the brain and have no permanence or ability to affect a person's thought or behaviour.

Awakening to the facet of mind also uncovers the difference between thinking and awareness. The Seeker is no longer fooled by the products of the brain and becomes aware that their thinking and feeling is separate from their awareness or consciousness. For instance, after fully awakening to the mind, the Seeker is able to watch feelings and emotions in their own mind without being drawn into them and is able to observe the feelings and emotions from their beginning all the way through their entire life-cycle to their complete and total end, without letting their judgment be affected by them.

At this stage, the Seeker also becomes aware of the ego and its function in the human mind. However, it must be pointed out that most Seekers will not understand the entire range and size of their ego until they fully awaken to the facet of self.

For most, awakening to the mind represents a revolutionary transformation. One no longer defines oneself through what they feel. This doesn't mean that the Awakened person does not have feelings or emotions; the body and the mind still create anger, hate, jealousy, greed, lust and guilt, etc., but rather than influencing the judgment of the person, it is the person themselves that decides what impact, if any, their feelings and emotions should have in any life situation.

To the fully Awakened person, all emotions become highly useful tools that can help them to become aware of unsolved wounds or traumas within themselves, or that they may be falling back to past conditioning.

The Facet of Self

Seekers awakening to this facet gradually or suddenly become aware of their ego in its totality, which was seen and thoroughly understood by Buddhism several thousand years ago, and modern science is only now catching up.

According to distinguished psychologist Carl Jung, the ego represents the conscious mind as it makes up the thoughts, memories, and emotions that a person is aware of. The ego is mostly responsible for feelings of identity and continuity in time. In its simplest form, ego is simply complete identification with form – thought forms, physical forms and emotional forms, though in his book titled A New Earth: Awakening to your life's purpose, Eckhart Tolle correctly points out that the ego identifies with thought forms the most:

> "In normal everyday usage, "I" embodies the primordial error, a misperception of who you are, an illusory sense of identity. This is

the ego. This illusory sense of self is what Albert Einstein ...referred to as "an optical illusion of consciousness." That illusory self then becomes the basis for all further interpretations, or rather misinterpretations of reality, all thought processes, interactions, and relationships. Your reality becomes a reflection of the original illusion."

Tolle continues:

"The ego identifies with having, but its satisfaction in having is a relatively shallow and short-lived one. Concealed within it remains a deep-seated sense of dissatisfaction, of incompleteness, of "not enough." "I don't have enough yet," by which the ego really means, "I am not enough yet ..." The ego perceives life through the lens of duality. Duality is the opposite of reality — it is the division of life into opposing forces such as love/hate, good/bad, right/wrong and holy/sinful..."

Tolle wisely advises that "if one can recognize illusion as illusion, it dissolves. The recognition of illusion is also its ending. Its survival depends on our mistaking it for reality. In the seeing of who we are <u>not</u>, the reality of who you <u>are</u> emerges by itself."

The ego is the root of all suffering. It is judgment, hatred and greed, and it grows when combined with ignorance. We love some foods and hate others. We want to be around some people, while avoiding others. We want our hair to be a certain way, and when it is not, the ego flares and shouts "This is not me!"

Ego is responsible for everything that is "wrong" with the world. Murder, rape, theft, war, poverty, mental illness and the purposeful destruction of our planet for profit...all of these are a direct result of the ego and the illusion of duality that we are separate from everyone and everything.

I remember when I awoke to my larger ego. A friend of mine was struggling, as many around the world were during the COVID pandemic, and I got the idea to travel and stay with him and his family for a while, figuring that I could help out somehow just by being there.

Before going, I checked in with my spiritual advisor to get his sense of the good intentions of my plan, and to ask him for any advice he may have. After listening and asking questions for about thirty minutes, he said that he approved of the plan in principle, but as I was leaving the meditation centre, he stopped me at the door and said something like, "Guard your expectations. You are so sure that you will be able to help this family. Your ego seems to be leading your expectations of what you will be able to do. You need to check it."

Standing there and staring into his kind eyes, my world simply shattered. I had always thought that I understood what ego was. To me, the ego was responsible for things like me worrying about how much I weighed, my overinflated sense of my professional worth and my extensive wardrobe of snappy sports jackets and ties. Upon hearing those words though, the monstrous vastness of my full ego truly   and completely became crystal clear to me. And it was horrifying. In an instant, perception shifted, and I completely and wholly understood for the first time that what I had always thought was my entire ego was merely the decoy that my real ego had put up to facilitate my continued blind duplicity in its grand delusion.

Meditating on and thinking about this for days and days, I came to understand that any judgment that my mind had ever made about another person was in fact my ego; my friend is overweight and needs to diet; it is better for my daughter to take ballet instead of gymnastics; I need to stay in this relationship because I can help my partner with her anxiety; my father should find a partner and travel more before old age sets in; I will be able to help my friend out of his current life challenges. Ego, ego, ego, ego, ego, ego. This was my mind telling me that I knew what was best for others in order to trick me into actively taking part in the shaping my world around me as my ego directed.

Once I had integrated these truths, the result was freedom. I understood that I no longer needed to have an opinion on the lives of any other person. Their life was their life, and it was each person's God given right to decide what was best for them. Each person is living their own life, trying to learn or remember the truths that will set us all free. Me having any opinion of what was better for any other person was simply me possibly interfering in their progress on their path of awakening to spiritual enlightenment.

With the realization of the ultimate truth of ego, all

attachments fell away from me. I realized that materialism and self-identifications like "My body is me", "I am male", "I am a Buddha-Dharma practitioner", "I'm a civil servant", "I'm a good son" and "people respect me" where simply attachments to the world that my ego had developed over my lifetime in order to ensure that my world around me was arranged optimally for my comfort and survival.

When a Seeker is able to see past their ego and all of their attachments fall away, they are able to separate thinking and awareness, and with that, the Awakened person completely ceases to suffer altogether, in that they completely and permanently enter a state of mind of total and complete acceptance to all that is, the present moment, without choosing between moments, or preferring one moment over another.

The now Awakened person is able to truly take responsibility for their entire life and everything that has happened in it. They no longer blame others for their past suffering, understanding now that suffering is a product of the ego. The Awakened person no longer tries to force their thinking on any other person, understanding that everyone is already making the best decisions that they are able to in the present moment, and that we all are responsible for our own learning and inner growth.

After integrating these new understandings into daily life, the Seeker usually loses all concern with forms (emotional, physical and thought). They become confident and a deep and powerful sense of self-worth blooms into permanent existence. Their need for the old style of relationships changes and they no longer desire to fit in or be "normal", and they allow themselves to be exactly who they are without the need for approval or acceptance from anyone.

The Awakened Seeker's personality may undergo a shift which may be noticeable to those around them to varying degrees. A common misunderstanding here is that an Awakened person's personality changes upon Awakening or enlightenment, but this is not accurate. A person that has fully awakened to the facet of self will have the same personality after as before, minus any character or personality traits that were not wholesome or did not move the person along the path to spiritual enlightenment.

Gone is the desire to, or automatic habit of, fitting into "normal" society, or of being politically correct, or yielding to authority. Rather, the Seeker now makes decisions based off of what is best for themselves and for all others involved in any situation, rather than what their ego wants. Constantly chasing happiness ends as the Seeker now understands that nothing outside of themselves can make them happy.

The Facet of Spiritual Energy

Basically speaking, spiritual energy is universal energy that flows into and through the human body through various points. When a Seeker Awakens to the existence of spiritual energy, which is also known as qi, prana, chakras or kundalini energy, changes will occur on the physical, mental and spiritual levels. Ancient practices such as Tai Chi, yoga, meditation and tantra can help to awaken this energy, which can happen gradually or all at once, just like any other Awakening.

Jon Darrall-Rew, European Director of the Global Purpose Movement and co-founder of Synergy Forum, explains what happens to a Seeker during this facet of Awakening:

> "Suddenly there is a new voltage of energy that is released within their body and mind and that begins to circulate through their being. This might be temporary or permanent, but energetic openings like this

often dramatically open someone up to new levels of consciousness, embodiment, and energetic intensity."

In his fascinating book titled <u>Reality Unveiled: The Hidden Keys of Existence That Will Transform Your Life (and the World)</u>, author Ziad Masri gives a scientific example of the power of spiritual energy:

"We're told that water is an inanimate element, something that exists as separate and apart from us, and which can only be changed if put through some kind of machine or chemical process. However, in the mid 1990s Dr. Masaru Emoto, a Japanese scientist, decided to see whether thoughts, words, and music could have any effect on water...Dr. Emoto's method involved showing words to water, showing pictures to water, playing music to water and praying to water. After that, he froze the water and then observed the frozen crystals under the microscope.

Now, if you told most people that you were showing a word or picture to water, they might think you were crazy. But what Dr. Emoto found was nothing short of astounding. The following image (from balagulmobin.org) is the result of water simply being thought at:

This is all the same water with the only difference being the word or phrase that was being thought at it. As logical, rational human beings, we've always been taught that inanimate objects and elements can't change their form based on thoughts and words. This is impossible in a Newtonian version of the world. The water is supposed to exist distinctly apart from us. It is supposed to have its own separate existence, and it is not supposed to be alive in any way to respond to thoughts and words like humans can. And yet, the evidence is as clear as day. It does respond. In fact, it responds more directly and beautifully than any one of us could have ever imagined by changing its very structure to reflect the energy of the words or thoughts."

After Awakening to the facet of spiritual energy, a Seeker may develop a higher sense of their environment, increased productivity at work and greater emotional balance as even further separation from ego happens over time.

The Facet of Universal Consciousness

"To those who experience this state; no

proof is required, for those who have not yet experienced this state; no proof will suffice..." - Leland Lewis

Universal Consciousness comes from the source of all life, which some refer to as cosmic intelligence, the Source, God, Allah, the Great Spirit and so forth. Human Consciousness comes from the Universal Consciousness, and so one can never be separate from it, but humans do not know this until they awaken. Universal Consciousness exists across the entire cosmos, or all of space and time, though Universal Consciousness exists outside of time and space. Perhaps it can best be described as the unknowable intelligence behind and guiding the evolution of what humans view as the physical universe.

When Awakening to Universal Consciousness, either gradually over time or in a great explosion from within, Human Consciousness expands to touch the whole world, and to even touch the stars.

A Seeker gains new understanding about the nature of reality and may feel an infusion of love or wisdom. If they have not done so as the result of Awakening to another facet, duality concepts such as good and bad dissolve completely, and the Seeker understands that inside every person, every tree, every rock, every planet, every galaxy, every particle of light and every moment in time is simply pure love.

Seekers who Awaken fully to this facet understand that there is no meaning or purpose to life itself. Love for life and everyone and everything in it springs from within the heart of the Seeker, and they find great happiness in their reconnection to everyone and everything.

If they have not already, a Seeker will lose all fear of death at this stage, and their sole focus becomes living in the present moment. When Human Consciousness is seen as surviving the physical body, fear of the loss of the body ceases to be a constant worry. Time and distance go back to simply being human concepts as the Seeker understands that they are just ways of thinking to help humans measure change and relative physical location.

Lastly, the Seeker is filled with the comprehension that the entire universe is connected and that trees, plants, rocks, the human body, planets and stars all consist of the same materiel, and all material originally came from the same place.

The Source, or God.

The Facet of True Reality

"Seeing is believing" is one of those sayings that supports what is perhaps the biggest of all the things that humans have misunderstood at one point or another, that our reality around us is exactly and only what we see through our eyes.

But it is not. Not even close.

Science tells us that the human eye can only see

0.005% of existing energy waves called "visible light". Which means that 99.995% of light is not visible to the human eye. Astronomers and astrophysicists estimate that only 4% of the universe is viewable to the naked eye or any other current technology, the other 96% thought to be "dark matter" or "dark energy" that is not yet detectable.

Also consider the basic building block for everything in our universe, the atom. It is generally accepted that our universe is about fourteen billion years old, though some theories place the age at much older than that. All of the carbon, nitrogen and oxygen atoms in our galaxy, in our solar system, on this planet and in our bodies were created in stars older than our sun.

The human body is literally made of star material.

But if one looks very closely at an atom through the lens of quantum physics, they learn that 99.9999999999996% of the atom is simply empty space. The core of the atom seems to be solid, but it is infinitely small, and most of the space in the atom is completely empty of anything. The solid matter that we feel when we touch an atom, or rather an incomprehensibly large number of atoms, comes purely from the electrostatic repulsion between the atoms. That book or tablet that you are holding? You are not really holding it. It is floating between your fingers. That chair you are sitting on? You are actually hovering one 100-millionth of a centimetre above it.

This is what is meant by "true reality". What we humans see in our mind through our five senses as reality around us and right in front of our noses, is only the smallest piece of what is really there. Human beings only have the equipment to detect the tiniest part of the true reality around us and throughout the universe.

When a person begins to open their mind and deeply understand these ideas or concepts, they begin to Awaken to the fifth facet.

While the five stages of Awakening are always completed in order, even when they are completed "instantaneously" or in milliseconds, the facets of Awakening can be developed in any order, speed or level relative to each other. Being awake to one facet may help awaken the Seeker to another facet, while other facets have no relation at all. For example, a Seeker can be partially or even fully awakened to the nature of reality, while only being partially or wholly unawakened in one or more of the other facets. Such a person might tend to work in astronomy and quantum physics.

Chapter 4: Enlightenment

"Your own Self-Realization is the greatest service you can render the world." - Ramana Maharshi

What does it mean to be Enlightened?

A key issue that many minds have raised with trying to describe what happens when someone becomes fully enlightened is that there is no language known to man that can convey ultimate realization, or ultimate truth, or the true nature of humans, societies, the world, the universe or of reality itself.

One can only convey concepts or ideas that are man-made and so are imperfect and flawed. Adyashanti explains it best in his book titled The End of Your World:

> "The problem with defining [enlightenment] is that upon hearing each of these descriptions, the mind creates another

100

image, another idea of what this ultimate truth or ultimate reality is all about. As soon as these images are created, our perception is distorted once again. In this way, it's really impossible to describe the nature of reality, except to say that it's not what we think it is, and it's not what we've been taught it is. In truth, we are not capable of imagining what it is that we are. Our nature is literally beyond all imagination."

Despite this, we must start with a common understanding of enlightenment, and taking a good sampling of existing information and applying our Filter, the following definition is produced:

Full spiritual enlightenment or "Enlightenment" is the highest state of consciousness, or of being, that is possible for a human to attain. Feelings, emotions, the self, the body and concepts of the human mind cease to have any affect on the judgment of the person who lives fully in the present moment, understands the very nature of reality itself and everything in it, and whose sole purpose is Truth.

Enlightenment is the grand finale of all Awakenings after which the person sees and fully comprehends on a very deep level the truth in everything, or the nature of reality and everything in it. Awareness of their environment grows, and they develop clear and definite purpose in everything that they do. Adyashanti describes it as "a profound return to our essence, to the simplicity of what we are, and is a state of naturalness and ease".

Enlightenment has also been described as "dying into the ordinary". The Enlightened person no longer struggles against any part of life, now deeply understanding that they were not seeing true reality before, and that their responses to the world around them had come mainly from fear, greed and ignorance. They arrive at a natural state of being, an unaltered state of consciousness, or pure consciousness.

What is the main difference between Awakening and Enlightenment? Bonnie Greenwell, PhD, offers this:

> "The difference between awakening and enlightenment is that an awakened being knows the truth, and the enlightened person has surrendered everything to it and simply lives within it."

The Stages of Enlightenment

An Unawakened person becomes a Seeker when they experience their first full or partial spiritual awakening, regardless of the facet of awakening and whether or not the person realized or understood what happened to them at the time. Since Awakening leads to full spiritual enlightenment, any Seeker that has had at least a partial Awakening can then be considered to be on the path to full spiritual enlightenment and could be considered at least partially Enlightened.

Most authorities on the subject provide a similar sense of the different stages that a Seeker will pass through during the entire process of enlightenment, from the very first awakening until full spiritual enlightenment, or Salvation, also known as Nirvana. In the same way that Awakening is a process that can take milliseconds, decades or anywhere in between to complete fully, so to is Enlightenment a process that takes varying numbers of rotations around the sun to fully mature.

Applying our Filter to our sampling, we come up with the following list of the different stages associated with the journey to Enlightenment, and most closely resembles some found in Hinduism:

1. Seeking: In this initial stage, an Unawakened person is about to have, is having, or has just had an Awakening. It is often described as a pure desire to seek out

ultimate truth and cleanse the mind of misconceptions that the person believes to be reality, but which are the result of tribal conditioning.

This stage can be marked by a lowering in materialism, and has four sub-stages:

- Duality: The Seeker starts understanding the deep relationship between good and bad, permanent and impermanent and real and unreal, and begins to view each as a single concept, rather than two separate and independent concepts.

- Mindfulness: The Seeker starts to lose interest in temporary things and emotional, physical and thought forms.

- Suffering: The Seeker achieves mastery over the six senses – taste, touch, smell, vision, hearing and the

105

sense of intuition. When this sub-stage is realized, the Seeker gains mastery over their senses and stops reacting to objects perceived through these senses.

- ○ Seeking: This is the final sub-stage wherein the Seeker develops the willingness or desire to achieve Enlightenment.

2. Self Inquiry: At this stage, a deep desire to find the right teaching and information blossoms within the Seeker, who will reflect on the past and present in search of potential answers. The person turns inward at this stage, often taking up a mindfulness practice.

3. Materialism: At this stage, the Seeker attains a threadlike state of mind, cultivating and deepening their indifference to material objects. More wholesome life purpose often

106

develops.

4. Consciousness: At this stage, the Seeker gains full mastery of the mind and all worldly desires fall away.

5. Detachment: At this stage, the Seeker achieves complete detachment from forms.

6. Universal Consciousness: In this stage, the Seeker finally sees and understands the truth of reality and comes to completely understand that the soul is the permanent and actual self.

7. Enlightenment: Also known as the state of super-consciousness, this state is complete and permanent enlightenment. The Seeker is freed from all the behavioural tendencies or karmic imprints which influenced the person in the past and is completely freed from the ideas of duality.

As one progresses through the stages of

Enlightenment, their vibration increases, awareness grows and the person gets an ever-increasing understanding of what it is to be part of a species, yet also a separate self, and how they fit into the universe.

Once any Seeker fully and completely understands and integrates of all of the ultimate truths required to complete all five facets of Awakening, they become Enlightened, that is to say, they become a fully spiritually enlightened being, just like, but not the same being as, Buddha, Jesus, and Muhammad.

The Enlightened being is no longer a prisoner of perception in any way. They deeply understand that what their mind tells them they are experiencing through their senses is not the truth of reality. Only an Enlightened being can see the truth of all things at all times, which they can see or sense clearly in everything and everyone around them.

The Enlightened being no longer does anything out of obligation or need, but instead they are guided through inspiration and desire for wholesomeness in all things. Their direct connection to all of life deepens, and they are often inspired to create or live in a whole new manner. Life purpose dissolves and they instead live their Truth.

Chapter 5: The Target State

Introduction

The term "target state", given all of the previous information so far, is that state of consciousness in which an Enlightened being could be expected to live every day. This is not to suggest that every Enlightened being lives exactly the same way, but rather that in examining what the literature has told us about awakening and enlightenment so far, one can find many commonalities with which to draw some reasonable conclusions about how an Enlightened person might approach everyday life.

For example, spiritual scientist, teacher, and author Thomas Vazhakunnathu provides a simple version of such a target state when he looks at what traits an enlightened being would likely display in everyday life:

- Blissfulness: The ability to experience love, oneness, freedom, gratitude, peace and happiness continuously without any external stimulus.

- Mindfulness: An increased awareness and focus on the present moment.

- An Abundant Life: Such a person attracts people and opportunities that align with their Truth.

- A Powerful Mind: Enlightened people can appear to be very focused, intelligent, intuitive, sensitive and positive.

- A Balanced Personality: They would have very good to excellent self-control, confidence, contentment and detachment, and would not be easily surprised or bothered by circumstances.

- Increased Health and Well-being: Most Enlightened people can be expected to possess relative general good physical and mental health, and they may even age at a slower rate.

- A Sense of Immortality: There is a total loss of fear of death.

Just the same way as Vazhakunnathu gathers traits that an enlightened being would display in order to give us a slightly better overall sense of such a person, the following sections will combine what historical and current minds, literature and followers of the big five have said how an enlightened being would think, act and generally live life in society.

Passing all through our Filter and adding context information and modern language where appropriate for clarity, the following is a list of views, traits and approaches to life that an Enlightened person would most likely display in differing amounts.

Before we begin, the reader is asked to keep in mind that despite what some may claim, there is no blueprint for exactly how an Enlightened being would think, how they would make decisions, how they would act and interact socially, and how such a being would live life day to day. What is presented in the following pages is merely for the reader's consideration.

The Body

An Enlightened person would know that they are privileged to experience life only because of the most amazing biological machine in the universe, the human body. The body is made up of roughly thirty trillion cells, which is a lot more than the number of stars in the entire universe, and the human brain is estimated to be able to make a billion billion calculations per second.

That are a lot of moving parts, and an Enlightened person would have a strong sense that the health of the human body and mind is vital to their life experience. However, abnormalities of the body, usually referred to as physical challenges, would not directly prevent any person from attaining Enlightenment, though there may be indirect effects, such as impeding one's ability to travel, to access buildings, to read or receive data via one of the five senses, etc.

Common methods used by Enlightened people to maximize the health of the physical body are likely to include:

Physical Practices

An Enlightened person will very likely engage in some sort of wholesome physical practices that involve all the muscles in the body, such as yoga or Tai Chi, though any type of physical exercise can be used, including arm-curling soup cans. Normally, the amount of and intensity of the exercise is only enough to maintain what the person considers to be optimum health, which would differ from person to person.

Most commonly though, if their body is healthy and strong enough, Enlightened people would likely use it as their main mode of transport, such as walking, jogging, cycling or rollerblading most everywhere that they go and far into old age.

An Enlightened person would likely have a surprisingly deep understanding of the muscle groups, internal organs and workings of the human body, as this is needed to fully awaken to the facet of spiritual energy. Among other things, awakening to this facet awakens a person to the different points of energy (called "Chakras") within the body and how they affect and are affected by our mind, our reality and our view of reality.

Enlightened people that are "physically challenged" will have no social concern whatsoever for their physical circumstance. They will always be completely at ease with their body, and they will have a knack for making other people feel at ease as well. Enlightened people would <u>all</u> understand that we are not our bodies and that everything in creation, including the human body, is perfection in expression, both beautiful and always radiating pure love within and without.

An Enlightened person will also be perfectly at ease with people of any body type and size, physical abnormality, injury, illness or disease or state of physical or mental health, including corpses and the clinically insane, and make no judgment whatsoever about any such person or their life.

All they would see is a perfect human being.

<u>Wholesome Eating</u>
An Enlightened being would understand that old adage "you are what you eat" perhaps better than anyone, for they would have a deep awareness of the relationship between food, the body and

optimum physical, mental and spiritual health. But one would not typically expect to see such a person following any particular diet, though an Enlightened person would usually be quite aware of exactly what they were eating and drinking and how they could be affected on all levels.

The Enlightened person would likely tend to eat more wholesome, natural foods and would generally avoid processed foods of all types. They would tend not to be over-eaters or overweight, and in fact most would often consume far less than the Unawakened. This does not mean that they would never pig out, or that they would never eat sweets, just when they did, they would most likely take a "middle of the road", 80/20 or other reasonable and wholesome approach to their food consumption.

Enlightened people do not suffer from food addictions, as any form of mental illness typically prevents Awakening and Enlightenment until it is completely understood, at which point it ceases to have any affect on that person.

Judgment Impairing Substances

While all of the big five has different types of rules or restrictions on drinking alcohol and using other substances that both impair judgment and affect state of consciousness, an Enlightened being makes their own decision as to whether or not they use such substances and for what purposes.

Such a being may drink alcohol a little or a lot, or may smoke tobacco or cannabis, or use psychoactive mushrooms and LSD, or may do none of these. Or may suddenly stop or start such behaviour. However, an Enlightened person will never intentionally use any substance in an unwholesome manner, or cause others to do so.

As with food addictions, Enlightened people do not suffer from substance abuse, addiction or other forms of mental illness. That does not mean that anyone that suffers from an addiction or mental illness cannot become Enlightened in the future, it just means that they will not be able to attain Enlightenment until they completely understand the addiction, what it is, what its root causes are and how it affects and has affected their mind, body and spirit.

At that point, the addiction ceases to have any affect on the person.

Pain, Injury, Illness & Disease
An Enlightened person would still be very human, and so their body would remain subject to pain, injury, illness and disease, but their judgment would not be affected, unless that was a side effect of the illness, treatment or any medication used in the treatment.

The Mind
The Enlightened person understands on a core level that they are not their mind, for they would understand the nature of self and no-self. They

would likely view the human brain as a receiver of consciousness and the soul's link to the body, and that the brain is responsible for everything that they perceive about life, the world and existence itself. Any Enlightened being would understand how their brain works on a very detailed level, even though they may not have any formal education on the subject or may not be able to communicate it effectively to another person.

Intelligence

A common misperception about Enlightenment is that all Enlightened people are highly intelligent, or that a person can only awaken and attain full spiritual enlightenment if the person has a certain IQ level. While that certainly may seem so much of the time, Enlightened people are just more fully aware of what they know and what they don't know, and only speak when it is both wholesome and appropriate to do so.

Claiming IQ matters in Awakening and

Enlightenment is merely another form of tribalism. Being of "low IQ" does not mean that one cannot learn or understand on a very deep level the complex concepts key to Awakening and Enlightenment, it simply means that it will take the person more energy to do so, either in terms of effort and/or time. "High IQ" and "low IQ" are simply mislabels for people that absorb and integrate information needed for learning at a faster and micro-leaning (small/focused picture thinkers) rate, and those people that absorb and integrate the exact same information at a slower and macro-leaning (big-picture thinkers) rate.

It would be more helpful to humanity in general for it to stop discriminating between low and high intelligence. Every human being has the same human brain model with the exact same capacity to become Enlightened, the only variable being the rate that different people learn. Some brains absorb information "instantly", and all others require a period of time to absorb that same information, which naturally differs from brain to brain.

It should also be noted that most if not all intellectual information on the subjects of awakening and enlightenment is not designed to be absorbed by people that absorb information extremely slowly, so even when such people do locate and/or gain access to such information, they are not able to comprehend and/or absorb much of it, if any at all. Even a person with a learning disability such as Down's Syndrome or other similar condition can become Enlightened, given enough time, well-designed learning concepts and the necessary environmental support.

Mental Illness

Mental illness of any kind is a barrier to awakening to the facets of mind and self, and so a person that is Enlightened will not suffer from any chronic mental illness that affects their ability to be completely honest with themselves, as this is a prime ingredient in true spiritual growth and evolution and is required in order to exercise wholesome judgment.

Acute mental illness can occur normally in both the Unawakened and in Seekers, as feelings like depression and anxiety can actually be signs of an impending Awakening. However, upon Awakening fully, any such acute mental illnesses would cease completely and permanently, except in the case where the Seeker goes through further Awakenings.

Chronic or recurring mental illness in adulthood is generally an indicator of unaddressed childhood trauma, and any Enlightened person by definition will be free of any ongoing mental illness, as this is necessary to fully Awaken to the facets of mind and self. The Awakened person may have self-healed from their childhood traumas, or they may have been helped by mental health professionals and/or mental health support groups.

An Enlightened person may have suffered from addictions in the past, but upon Awakening to the facets of mind and self, any addiction would have either instantly or gradually ceased to affect the person, who would then permanently remain free of addiction for the rest of their life, except perhaps in the event of extreme mental trauma, though no such extreme occurrences were located while researching this book.

Any mental illness that affects a person's ability to be completely honest with themselves and that occurs as a result of environmental factors will prevent Awakening and Enlightenment until remedied sufficiently.

Any mental illness that affects a person's ability to be completely honest with themselves and that occurs as a result of genetic factors will prevent Awakening and Enlightenment in this lifetime, unless resolved through advances in medical science, other relevant sciences or other means.

<u>Ego</u>

The Enlightened person would be highly familiar with the ego in general and their ego specifically. They would understand on a very deep level that the ego is a vital function of the human brain and is necessary for any human being to mature from birth to a physical and intellectual level needed to remain healthy and alive in the world and function successfully within societies.

An Enlightened person would understand that the ego must not repressed or ignored, but understood deeply and welcomed as a friend, for the ego is our only true fan and supporter, and once a person has fully Awakened to their ego, it no longer has any influence on the judgment and actions of that person. Most Enlightened people would likely view the ego as highly useful that tells them when they need to focus on themselves.

<u>Feelings & Emotions</u>

Similar to the ego, feelings and emotions would

likely be highly useful tools to a person that is Enlightened. They would never be suppressed, but rather carefully noted and observed whenever they arose, which an Enlightened person would likely do so often that it would eventually become automatic and happen mostly in the background of their awareness.

Finally, an Enlightened person may consider their feelings and emotions to be their ego communicating important information to them, and among other things, would likely be used primarily to monitor mental health and to sense intention in others.

Concepts

An Enlightened person that has awakened to both the facets of mind and self would cease to be affected by human concepts such as time, distance, age, death, etc. They would still understand concepts and use concepts in everyday life, such as in teaching, but they would not be easily fooled or bound by any human concept.

The Now

While definitely one of the core concepts in an Enlightened person's toolbox, it is also one of the simplest to understand and apply for the Unawakened and Enlightened alike. Most modern writers on spirituality have a lot to say about the now, the present moment and mindfulness, but much of it is what can be referred to as spiritual fluff, for this concept of the present moment is often overfocused on and misses the mark completely.

Does focusing on the now and living more in the present moment really help to reduce depression, anxiety and other types of emotional and existential suffering? Yes, and much more, and there is much scientific data to support this. However, lost somewhere are the cold hard facts that this lessening in suffering is only a temporary side effect of the practice of mindfulness, not the mail goal, and that being in the present moment is only the first step of the longer awakening and enlightenment processes.

So, what is the truth then? Simply this; the lessening in suffering that most if not all people will feel as their mindfulness practice develops and they become able to be more present in their daily lives, instead of constantly reliving the past or agonizing about the future, is not a permanent lessening in the core suffering of the being, but rather more similar to how one's head stops hurting when one stops constantly banging it against a wall.

Living in the past, such as reliving past traumas and regretting past decisions are simply tools of the ego used to bind the person to their identity, strengthening the delusion that the Unawakened are the sum of all their successes and failures as defined by their tribal conditioning.

Agonizing about the future is exactly the same thing; it is the sleight of hand of the ego designed to keep the person's attention off of the now and focused on what the ego wants the person to do to maintain or improve their standing in the collective delusion of the society.

When any person stops or reduces the amount of time that they spend living in the future or the past, they are not actually feeling an increase in happiness, they are merely feeling less suffering, but this is often misinterpreted.

Suffice it to say that the Enlightened person that lives entirely in the present moment does not do so to lessen their own suffering, which is the goal touted by many contemporary instructors of mindfulness. Instead, they do so because it is the natural state of being for a human being, the only state of being that provides the ultimate clarity required to see what is truly occurring in the present moment on every level of perception, with the single intention of reacting in line with their Truth.

When one lives in the present moment for an extended period of time, the suspension of suffering eventually normalizes and the person will begin to suffer again as undesired memories, feelings, emotions and urges again being to populate the mind. It is at this point that many Unawakened then begin to use mindfulness in an unwholesome way, as some seek to avoid the negative rather than focusing on it in order to determine its root causes.

This should not be taken to suggest that an Enlightened person does not plan for the future, for that would be delusional about the nature of the body. The body requires food, shelter and medicine when necessary, and in our world, these things generally must be hustled for. But an Enlightened person always lives fully in the present moment, unless they decide to engage the concept of time for the purposes of learning and planning, teaching, etc.

Furthermore, while Enlightened people may typically be inclined to keep up to date on world events, they mostly do so because of that big picture thinking that they are famous for. War, famine, politics, terrorism, entertainment; these things typically hold no interest for an Enlightened being, as they are always in perfect alignment with what is, and completely nonresistant to the present moment.

Distractions

An Enlightened person has awakened to the facets of mind and self and has seen through the veil of delusion that entertainment, consumerism, and social media have on the Unawakened. This does not mean that a person that is Enlightened would not engage in entertainment or social media or wouldn't buy things that would not be considered necessities of life, but rather if they choose to do so, they do so for a specific wholesome purpose.

Focus

An Enlightened person would have the ability to highly focus on an object, a vision in the mind, an ache in the body, or a personal or social issue with complete ease. This skill may have been developed over years of meditative study or other similar practice that promotes both deepening focus and expanding awareness, or it may have been attained instantly upon Enlightenment.

This ability to powerfully focus would most often be used to focus on the present moment. An Enlightened being would most often know more than anyone else present exactly what is going on in any given circumstance and would most likely be fully aware of the quantum number of potential possibilities that could occur in the next many moments. It is not that they know everything or can tell the future, but rather that the focus of an Enlightened being on the present moment would usually be so sharp that they could rarely be surprised by any occurrence or result.

Brain Health

Any Enlightened person will almost always engage in some practice or exercise that works the brain.

Just as they would need to be fully aware of the body and what it needs to maintain ideal physical, emotional and spiritual health (each person would define that for themselves), they would also likely be very familiar with the physical and mental aspects of the human brain and what it needs to stay healthy and functioning fully.

This practice would often be meditation or some form of it, but would not always be so. It is a common belief that all Enlightened beings regularly meditate. All can and most do, but it could be expected that some may prefer other forms of mental exercise, such as art and other forms of creation, strategy and pattern recognition games, and even sports or other activities that require a high degree of focus and concentration.

It has been often said that living fully in the present moment becomes the meditation of an Enlightened being.

Personality

The personality of an Enlightened person is perhaps the most difficult thing to talk about because really, an Enlightened person can display any type of personality or character they choose to, even ones that most might not expect.

For example, an Enlightened person may display anger, such as righteous anger at the needless and purposeful suffering of any living thing, or even everyday normal anger if the Enlightened person feels that displaying this emotion is the most wholesome thing to do in a given circumstance.

An Enlightened person may be rude or kind, generous or stingy, moody or calm, or any other combination of personality traits. The reader may recall that a person that has Awakened to both facets of mind and self still has feelings and emotions, but when they arise, the person most times instantly becomes aware of them and decides whether to allow them to influence their judgment or behaviour.

Enlightened people have no concern with breaking rules or disobeying authority, for rules and authority are simply concepts designed to facilitate or promote a behaviour or attitude in a group of people. But Enlightened people always make the most wholesome choice in nay situation, and if that choice conflicts with a rule or assertion of authority, then the Enlightened person will typically do what they judge to be most wholesome, which may mean breaking a rule or disobeying authority.

Relationships

Being highly genuine, empathetic and compassionate, an Enlightened person will often draw people to them, particularly children. But unlike the Unawakened, an Enlightened person does not define themselves by their relationships, nor do they unwillingly play any defined role in relationships.

Tribal labels such as son, spouse, mother, friend, etc. will have all fallen away and an Enlightened person, and they themselves would decide which type of role to fill, or which combination of roles, if any, and to what degree they would fill or not fill such roles.

In all relationships, the Enlightened being's primary purpose would be to promote the wholesome, while avoiding the unwholesome, either in themselves or another.

It would not be uncommon for an Enlightened person to leave the rest of humanity to their own journey and live in seclusion. Some Enlightened beings who feel no compunction to engage with the Unenlightened are known to separate themselves physically and/or geographically to varying degrees from former associates, friends, family, community and even humanity in general.

Personal Relationships

From birth, we welcome the imprint or conditioning of the tribe around us. From the day that we are born to the day that we partially or fully Awaken or become Enlightened, our sense of self-worth comes from how well we have integrated with the mass-delusions of tribe, culture and society. We don't buy an expensive watch, a fast car or a huge house because we need these things to survive in our environment, we buy them so that we fit in, so that others can see how successful we are, or at least how successful we want to appear to be.

Even if a person has been born with a physical defect or has experienced significance physical trauma in childhood or adolescence, how they view themselves will be a reflection of how those around that person view them. If the person is loved and told they are beautiful, that is what is believed growing up. If the person is outcast and laughed at or spit upon, their belief in their own value degrades accordingly.

However, any Enlightened being would understand that the most critical relationship in the life of any human being is the relationship that they have with themselves, their ego and their higher self; all other external relationships are merely a reflection of the health and abundance of the self-love within. Without first learning how to love oneself, one cannot truly know how to love another in a wholesome way.

As a result of this higher understanding, an Enlightened person has no need for the approval of anyone, nor would they be concerned about their public image or their place in society, their community and even their family. Its not that they would shirk responsibility, it is just that an Enlightened being cannot be defined or labelled by anyone or anything. It is the Enlightened being alone that determines what role, if any, that they fill in any aspect of social life.

Furthermore, Enlightened beings would not feel the

need to help every person they know or see to spiritually awaken. If specifically asked for information or teaching, it is generally provided if such is determined to be wholesome and appropriate. If the Enlightened being assesses that an Unawakened person may be in a position on their journey of Awakening and Enlightenment to be able to benefit from the introduction of a wholesome concept, they may plant a seed and leave it at that.

Else, attempting to awaken those who are not ready can be more harmful than helpful.

Teacher/Student Relationships

It is far from a rule, but it is not uncommon for an Enlightened person to take on the role of helping other beings awaken and attain enlightenment. Such a being is referred to in Buddhism as a Bodhisattva. A Bodhisattva is one who has attained enlightenment and chooses to devote themselves to the awakening and enlightenment of all other beings.

An Enlightened being will almost never provide their teachings without first being specifically requested by to do so, and would never take advantage of their students, or place a barrier to their teaching and knowledge, such as charging money, goods or services for their insights into the truth of reality itself.

It can be a sign of only partial Enlightenment for any being to charge money for their products or their teachings for the purpose of personal financial gain over what they need for a humble lifestyle. An exception here would include the covering of travel and administrative costs for the teachings of an Enlightened person, as such beings can often be in great demand around the world as thirst for spiritual knowledge seems to be increasing at a global rate.

However, when a student devotes themselves to the teachings of an Enlightened being, their suffering immediately begins to lessen, and they begin to go through the levels and facets of awakening at a greatly accelerated pace. Such students most often develop a great awe of, and a soul-crushing love and respect for, the Enlightened being that has most unselfishly given of themselves.

It is not uncommon for students of Enlightened beings to devote varying amounts of their income and other types of resources to help their spiritual teacher continue to live their Truth. Students will also engage in fundraising activities to support their teacher.

Sexual Relationships

Enlightened people still have all of the feelings, emotions and physical urges of the Unawakened, but their judgment simply is not affected by them. Sex is a natural and healthy human process, and an Enlightened person will engage in sexual activity if and when they assess it as wholesome and beneficial for all involved.

Understanding that love is love, the fully

Enlightened person will not be deluded or bound or influenced by any of the sexual discriminatory concepts or practices of any tribe, culture or society.

It can be an indication of only partial Enlightenment for any being to become sexually involved with a student. An exception here may include romantic partners.

Business Relationships

Unless an Enlightenment being is financially independent or living the life of a monk or an aesthetic, they are going to need to hustle to varying amounts for basic necessities like any other person. Enlightened beings would most often prefer to work independently, running their own business or providing wholesome services on a contractual basis.

Enlightened beings would typically earn their money through providing wholesome products or services, and would likely gravitate towards such vocations as physical, mental or spiritual healing including medicine, acupuncture, massage, midwifery, Reiki and Qigong. They would often be teachers of yoga, meditation, mindfulness, or other wholesome orthopraxies.

It would be hard to imagine any Enlightened being ever knowingly earning money through ventures that cause suffering to any living being directly or indirectly, or that harm nature or the environment.

When at work, the Enlightened would be highly likely to devote themselves completely to their task. They would rarely if ever be lazy, late or rushed, nor would they be likely to engage in workplace politics or gossip.

Relationship with Nature & the Environment

An Enlightened person would be deeply aware of humanity's dependant relationship with nature and flow with it effortlessly. They would often engage in practices that support or protect nature and the environment, such as recycling and using environmentally friendly cleaners, packaging and waste disposal.

As mentioned previously, Enlightenment beings have been known to seek to live separately from all or most of society and may prefer to live minimalistically in rural or deep country settings, or even aesthetically in forests and in caves. However, this is not the rule.

Enlightened people will often grow their own food, living either partially or completely off the land and taking and returning energy to it in a wholesome and sustainable manner. They would often vegetarian or vegan and would likely always be sure that their eating habits caused as little suffering as was reasonably possible in their unique living context.

Relationships with Animals
Animals, both wild and tame, would likely gravitate

to an Enlightened person, as animals would be able to feel the person's calmness, and they would likely be curious about the constant positive vibration within the person, their residence and even the land immediately around their residence, particularly if the person meditated regularly at that location.

It would not be surprising for an Enlightened person to kill an animal, such as a rat in the home, or when trapping a rabbit for food. The Enlightened person would understand the circle of biological life, and that by virtue of simply being alive, every living thing kills uncountable other living things every day in the simple growing, harvesting and digestion of food and other forms of energy.

God, the Soul & Death

God
Any Enlightened person will have transcended the human concept of God and would likely be of the view that most every religion around the world and

throughout history was the right path, if it led to Enlightenment even some of the time.

Most religions have similar ideas and beliefs and envision an all-knowing ultimate being that is pure love, but tribalism inevitably permeates all orthodoxy and orthopraxy, and so any religion can actually prevent full Enlightenment, unless the being is able to see past the tribalistic dogma to the ultimate truth of existence, God and the universe beyond.

An Enlightened being may choose to identify or not with any religion, dogma, orthodoxy or orthopraxy, as they understand that it is the destination that matters in matters of awakening and enlightenment, not the path.

To be clear, this is not to say that all Enlightened beings will chose a God or a religion, but rather that they are free to decide what their understanding and perception of God is and is not, and through whatever lens that they decide to utilize, any

Enlightened person will have completely resolved the issue of the higher being within their own hearts and minds.

An excellent revisionings of God is by Episcopal Bishop John Shelby Spong in his book <u>Why Christianity Must Change or Die</u>. In his book, the author acknowledges that the Christian concepts of God, heaven and hell and wholesome living must evolve, or the faith runs the risk of losing entire congregations who are no longer buying into the sometimes-ancient dogmas, and who may be seeking answers that make more sense in the light of modern science and thought.

<u>The Soul</u>

Similar to the issue of God, an Enlightened person will have resolved the issues of the eternity of the soul, life after death, resurrection and other forms of living again or living forever, as religion no longer controls development and spread of such information, and science has made quantum strides in the last many decades.

For example, Dr. Ian Stevenson was an American psychiatrist who worked for the University of Virginia School of Medicine for fifty years. He spent more than four decades interviewing more than 3,000 children who had very detailed and specific past-life memories. In conducting his research, Dr. Stevenson found that these children were not only able to recall their full name from a previous life, but they could also relate the names of past family members and friends, despite having absolutely no connection whatsoever to those people in their current life and living in completely different areas of the world.

Many children could also relate with uncanny accuracy how and where the person they claimed to be in their past life had died. Dr. Stevenson had collected and verified so much of this data that he published a book detailing it all in 2001 called <u>Children Who Remember Previous Lives: A</u>

Question of Reincarnation.

Additionally, in 1994, Psychologist Dr. Michael Newton published his now infamous book titled Journey of Souls: Case Studies of Life between Lives, and then published additional test cases and findings in 2000 in a follow-up book titled Destiny of Souls: New Case Studies of Life between Lives.

In these books, Dr. Newton presents his jaw-dropping research into what he termed "life between lives." Most readers will likely be familiar with past-life regression hypnosis, where a person is hypnotized and regressed in time by a trained professional until they pass the moment of their own birth and recall details of their past lives.

However, Dr. Newton took things one step further; he regressed his voluntary subjects back to a point where their soul existed in a space between lives. After collecting and comparing the reports of more than seven thousand clients, Dr. Newton found that it did not matter if the client was atheist, ultra-religious or anything in between. Once they were in the proper hypnotized state where their conscious minds were effectively bypassed, their reports of what they saw and experienced were eerily consistent.

Reports from people around the world, from different cultures and tribal beliefs and all completely unaware of what others had reported, consistently indicated that upon the death of the physical body, there is absolutely no loss in consciousness whatsoever. Instead, the being experiences themselves as a soul with full awareness rising out of the body and continuing to exist seamlessly outside of it. Eventually the soul is drawn out of the Earth's plane, with many reporting seeing a tunnel of light to the spirit world where they are met by all of their loved ones that has passed on before them, not necessarily because they were missed, which they were, but largely to facilitate the recently deceased soul's transition from the trauma of death to the spirit realm.

Each research subject reported that they were an eternal soul visiting our material realm for the specific purpose of learning about life, love, greed, suffering, old age and death, and that the specific lessons that they sought to learn in each incarnation were intentionally selected by that very soul ahead of time and prior to being born.

Dr. Newton himself passed away in 2016, but not before co-founding the Society for Spiritual Regression and establishing The Newton Institute (TNI) for the study of life between lives hypnotherapy in the United States of America. TNI claims a current membership of Life Between Lives (LBL) certified therapists spanning twenty-six countries.

Other highly respected therapists who have published findings that support the work of Dr. Newton include Brian Weiss and Delores Cannon.

Other existential views are equally possible and likely in an Enlightened person.

Death

Simply, an Enlightened being, while still able to feel the physical emotion of fear through the body, fears neither death nor dying because they are in constant alignment with the present moment and completely nonresistant to reality as it happens. Whether they subscribe to the permanence of the soul, or they believe that their consciousness returns to the source of all being upon death, things like old age, sickness, disease, pain, death and dying would all be viewed as natural processes that every being who ever draws breath must experience first-hand.

They are the prices that we all must pay for experiencing life.

A fully Enlightened being would not fear death, nor likely any manner of death, nor would they have any real fear of the diseased or the dying, for they would ultimately be aware of, and empathetic, to all nuances of the human condition.

Goals & Life Purpose

Goals

The short- and long-term goals of an Enlightened person would pretty much be the same as any Unawakened. While success means nothing to the Enlightened, they may want to buy a house, get a new job, buy a fast car, learn a new skill, etc. Money would become simply a highly useful tool in the realization of wholesome goals for the Enlightened person, rather than a sole pursuit or security blanket. Whether an Enlightened person has lots of money or no money at all would be the decision of the Enlightened person themselves.

The only differences between the goals of the Enlightened and the Unawakened are the intentions behind those goals. In the Enlightened person, the purpose behind any goal will most always be of the most wholesome nature, and at minimum will not be unwholesome in any way.

As the reader is already aware, a very common

indicator of partial Enlightenment is being awake to the facets of spiritual energy, universal consciousness and and/or the truth of reality, while not being completely awake to the facet of self and the hidden ego. Such a partially Enlightened person may develop a genuine desire to help those around them, and even to help the entire world itself to awaken. However, when making their information available, they put up barriers to access to the information, such as charging an unreasonable amount of money.

No person who is fully Enlightened seeks to Awaken all those that they meet, for they understand that no one can be awakened by an outside force, each person can only awaken themselves.

If asked for teaching, no Enlightened person will charge any currency or service, for they fully understand that Enlightenment is the ultimate human right, and that charging anything would only serve as a barrier to the information and would stand in the way of Awakening and Enlightenment.

No Enlightened person will stand in the way of any other person's Awakening or Enlightenment.

It is not uncommon though for Enlightened beings to solicit and accept donations which are freely given.

Life Purpose

Again, there is a lot of information available on what the life purpose of an Enlightened being is, or at least what others want it to be or think it should be. Unsurprisingly, much of this information comes directly from long established orthodoxies and orthopraxies, which as was previously asserted are all tribal in nature, regardless of the sincere intentions of leadership and administrators. As such, there can be little doubt that the life purposes of an Enlightened person envisioned by any orthodoxy or orthopraxy must serve the long term needs of organization that administers it, which generally is to spread its influence, and as such it would be sage of us to step back at this point and shift our focus somewhat to contemporary thought.

What many contemporary thinkers agree on is that every person has an inner purpose and an outer purpose, the inner purpose being to awaken and attain full spiritual enlightenment. Eckhart Tolle says it magically:

> "Your life has an inner purpose and an outer purpose. Inner purpose concerns Being and is primary. Outer purpose concerns doing and is secondary. Your inner purpose is to awaken. It is as simple as that. You share that purpose with every other person on the planet – because it is the purpose of humanity.

When a person attains their inner purpose, full spiritual enlightenment, they then begin to live their outer purpose, which is their own unique personal

Truth, and living their Truth becomes that person's life purpose. After that, whatever happens, happens, and the Enlightened person reacts almost instantly with complete nonresistance and the utmost wholesomeness, more commonly known as pure love.

Author and Ph.D. Bonnie Greenwell, in her book titled <u>The Awakening Guide: A Companion for the Inward Journey</u>, puts it this way:

> "This call to a spiritual search is much more than a search for the escape hatch out of the finality of dying, although it may seem to start that way. It is actually a call to living. An internal drive is inviting us to reverse our attention from external form to interior essence, in order to know who we truly are, and then to live as that."

These views differ from those generally offered by orthodoxy and orthopraxy. Almost across the board, we see orthodoxies and orthopraxies suggest that a fully enlightened being would be fully devoted to their practice or their church. This would not likely be the perception of an Enlightened being.

While an Enlightened person may certainly choose to directly or indirectly support any particular religion or way of life, they may also just as likely choose to leave all that behind. The reader will recall that an Enlightened person has transcended their orthodoxy or orthopraxy and seen the truth of reality completely free of any veil or delusion. Such a person understands that in terms of Awakening and Enlightenment, it is not the journey or the path that is important, but rather the goal, attaining full spiritual enlightenment. Orthodoxies and orthopraxies make the focus of the journey the path as a necessity of survival and proliferation. The Enlightened view does not discriminate between paths, as all end in Nirvana.

Another common "enlightened" purpose of life for the fully enlightened claimed by relevant types of organizations is that they work tirelessly for the benefit, healing, awakening and enlightenment of others. This is a stereotype and supports the survival and spread of orthodoxy and societal way of life, as organizational lore and law dictate how an enlightened person would live their life. Any person who wanted to be considered enlightened must devote themselves to helping others of their belief system in ways defined by that orthodoxy or orthopraxy.

To be clear, it is not being suggested that this behaviour of orthodoxy and orthopraxy to "editorialize" or add information specifically developed for the purposes of its survival and spread is negative or suspicious in any way, nor is it being suggested that such behaviour is a failure or shortcoming. Any human concept, including orthodoxy and orthopraxy, will first and foremost seek to keep itself alive. There is no existence without existence. The purpose of our discourse is not to insult, but to speak simple truths and let others discuss.

Suffice to say that each Enlightened person will define their outer purpose in their own way, in alignment with their own Truth.

The life purpose of any Enlightened person can never truly be known...unless they are asked.

Epilogue

By the time that we are born, we have already lived our entire existence, that time in the womb, yearning and fearing that we won't get what we yearn for. This is the quintessential property of what it is to be human.

By the time a person is an adult, they generally seek only two things in varying degrees to stop that yearning, happiness or power.

Few seek Enlightenment.

Given the planet's current existential paradigm, a highly likely eventuality is that our world will continue down the path of destruction until governments of the world awaken. Governments of the world will not awaken though until societies awaken, and societies will not awaken until awakening takes precedence in education, and awakening will not take precedence in education until education takes over the administration of awakening. Churches and religions will still do what they do, but public education would make enlightenment available to the world in a nondenominational, non-editorialized, and thus for more usable form for the rest of us.

As I have said before, I have no expectations for this book. I am not claiming that what I have produced here is in any way is final and ultimate truth, I merely present it as fodder for thought.

If you take away nothing else, I hope that you take away or at least consider this:

Question. Seek. Become.

This is the path of every human being from awakening to enlightenment and the full realization of their own Truth, both within themselves and within Existence.

Definitions & Terms

Awakening: a process involving at first spiritual unrest, then seeking, then healing, and finally the realizing of ultimate truth, or full awakening. There are many stages to awakening, and there are different types of awakenings that can occur together or completely separate from each other. Awakening may take place over several lifetimes, but can be completed in a single lifetime and may result in reaching full spiritual enlightenment

Conditioning: currently existing learned view, or understanding of reality, or a particular part of reality

Enlightenment: full spiritual enlightenment or "Enlightenment" is the highest state of consciousness, or of being, that is possible for a human to attain

Fully Awakened: a state of consciousness where an individual has fully integrated the ultimate truths of a particular facets of awakening into their daily life, but has not done so for all facets

Fully Enlightened: the super-state of consciousness where an individual has fully integrated the ultimate truths of all facets of awakening into their daily life

Orthodoxy: religion, or a way of believing

Orthopraxy: a way of living

Partially Awakened: a state of consciousness where an individual has only partially realized great truths, or has fully realized all great truths needs to awake to a particular facet of awakening, but has not yet fully integrated them into their daily life

164

Partially Enlightened: a state of consciousness where an individual has fully awakened to one or more of the facets of awaking, but has not yet fully awakened to them all

Seeker: a person that is undergoing the process of awakening to enlightenment, and who seeks ultimate truth

Sleeper: a person who has not yet started the process of awakening, also called Unawakened

Tribe: the people and community that were involved in the raising and educating of an individual from birth until adolescence

Triggers: things or events that cause the process of awakening to begin

Truth: The ultimate truth of a human being, their

authentic self. When one lives in alignment with their Truth, genuine love is created within and flows through their entire body. Truth becomes the life purpose of a fully spiritually enlightened person.

Unawakened: a person who has not yet started the process of awakening, also called a Sleeper

Unwholesome: that which hinders an individual's progress on the path of awakening to enlightenment, or that which puts up barriers to progress

Wholesome: that which helps an individual's progress on the path of awakening to enlightenment, or that which removes barriers to progress

Sources

Online Sources

https://www.newadvent.org/cathen/14254a.htm

http://uniqueself.com/wp-content/uploads/2012/07/The_Five_Great_Awaken ings.pdf

https://awaken.com/2019/08/5-different-types-of-spiritual-awakening/

https://chopra.com/articles/10-signs-of-spiritual-enlightenment-awakening

https://chopra.com/articles/the-5-stages-of-spiritual-awakening

https://chopra.com/articles/the-5-stages-of-spiritual-awakening

https://consciousreminder.com/2017/06/08/11-stages-awakening-person-go-achieving-enlightenment/

https://eckharttolle.com/eckhart-on-the-dark-night-of-the-soul/

https://ekam.org/5-awakenings/

https://epublications.marquette.edu/cgi/viewconten
t.cgi?article=1537&context=theo_fac

https://hackspirit.com/spiritual-awakening/

https://kwanumzen.org/teaching-
blog/2019/1/14/dont-know-no-problem

https://lonerwolf.com/ego-death/

https://medium.com/the-apeiron-blog/the-dark-
night-of-the-soul-understanding-amidst-the-
absence-of-meaning-3494cb193bc2

https://myspiritualshenanigans.blog/stages-of-a-
spiritual-awakening/

https://sunnahonline.com/library/purification-of-
the-soul/191-awakening

https://thomasvazhakunnathu.medium.com/7-
signs-of-an-awakened-or-spiritually-evolved-
person-29e993391c49

https://www.catholicireland.net/stages-in-spiritual-
evolution/

https://www.chakras.net/

https://www.christianitytoday.com/pastors/2015/m
arch-online-only/5-stages-of-spiritual-

awakening.html

https://www.learnreligions.com/empty-your-cup-3976934

https://www.livescience.com/32828-humans-really-made-stars.html

https://www.nanice.com/article/636/The-5-Stages-of-Awakening-Where-are-you/

https://www.realizedbygrace.org/post/7-stages-of-spiritual-awakening-according-to-varaha-upanishad

https://www.realizedbygrace.org/post/7-stages-of-spiritual-awakening-according-to-varahaupanishad

https://www.researchgate.net/publication/331000405

https://www.sanskritimagazine.com/spirituality/25-common-signs-of-spiritual-awakening/

https://www.sathyasai.org/sites/default/files/pages/ya/stp/2018/stp-study-circle-part-3-spiritual-energy-the-soul.pdf

https://www.schoolofcoachingmastery.com/coaching-blog/5-positive-psychology-findings-that-blowholes-in-the-law-of-attraction

https://www.spiritrestoration.org/life/what-happens-after-kundalini-awakening/

https://www.spiritualawakeningprocess.com/2016/10/shifting-perspectives-walking-through.html

https://www.thewayofmeditation.com.au/types-awakening

https://www.vipassana.com/resources/box/dhammajiva-sevenfactors-vf10p.pdf

https://www.whyislam.org/social-issues/spiritual-awakening/

https://www.wikipedia.com

Copyright Sources

A New Christianity For A New World: Why Traditional Faith Is Dying & How A New Faith Is Being Born (2002) – John Shelby Spong

A New Earth: Awakening to your life's purpose (2005) – Eckhart Tolle

Awakening the Buddha Within: Eight Steps to Enlightenment (1998) – Lama Surya Das

Biocentrism: How Life and Consciousness are the Keys to Understanding the True Nature of the Universe (2010) – Bob Berman, Robert Lanza

Destiny of Souls: New Case Studies of Life Between Lives (2000) – Michael Newton

Dropping Ashes on the Buddha: The Teachings of Zen Master Seung Sahn (1994) – Stephen Mitchell

Essential Tibetan Buddhism (1996) – Robert A. Thurman

Infinite Life: Awakening to Bliss Within (2005) – Robert Thurman

Journey of Souls: Case Studies of Life Between Lives (1994) – Michael Newton

Keeping the Peace: Mindfulness and Public Service (2005) – Thich Nhat Hanh

Learning About Spiritual Awakenings: 2 Young Crones Library Book 9 – Elizabeth Chapman

Reality Unveiled: The Hidden Keys of Existence That Will Transform Your Life (and the World) (2017) – Ziad Masri

Reconciliation: Healing the Inner Child (2006) – Thich Nhat Hanh

Spiritual Theory of Everything A Unique Blueprint to Discover the Origin and Purpose of Life, Awaken Your Consciousness and Lead a Blissful Life (2020) – Thomas Vazhakunnathu

The Awakening Guide: A Companion for the Inward Journey (2014) - Bonnie Greenwell, Ph. D

The Elegant Universe: Superstrings Hidden Dimensions And The Quest For The Ultimate (2010) – Brian Greene

The End of Your World: Uncensored Straight Talk on the Nature of Enlightenment (2010) – Adyashanti

The God Argument: The Case against Religion and for Humanism (2013) – A. C. Grayling

The Secret (2000) – Rhonda Byrne

The Spiritual Awakening Process (2019) – Aletheia
Luna and Mateo Sol

The Truth About Spiritual Enlightenment: Bridging
Science, Buddhism and Advaita Vedanta (2017) - P,
Shanmugam

The Unbound Soul (2019) – Richard L Haight

What the Buddha Taught: Revised and Expanded
Edition with Texts from Suttas and Dhammapada
(1974) – Walpola Rahula

Your Soul's Plan: Discovering the Real Meaning of
the Life You Planned Before You Were Born (2009)
– Robert Schwartz

Printed in Great Britain
by Amazon